ASTROLOGY

ASTROLOGY

THE PRACTICE OF CELESTIAL DIVINATION

MARION WILLIAMSON

SIRIUS

All illustrations courtesy of Shutterstock

SIRIUS

This edition published in 2024 by Sirius Publishing, a division of
Arcturus Publishing Limited,
26/27 Bickels Yard, 151–153 Bermondsey Street,
London SE1 3HA

ISBN: 978-1-3988-3605-1
AD011467UK

Printed in China

CONTENTS

INTRODUCTION

strology reveals infinitely more than whether you're a clumsy but optimistic Sagittarius or a sentimental, home-loving Cancer. At the moment of your birth, your unique character was captured in the heavens in the form of your birth chart. This book explains how to get to grips with the basics of astrology and will hopefully bring you a step closer to what could become a lifelong passion. The more you learn about the planets' intricate patterns and the meanings we have given them over thousands of years, the deeper astrology will get under your skin. The ancient truths revealed by the planets, and their beautifully complex interactions, will inspire you to understand yourself better and give sparkling insight into the character of the people around you. Soon you'll discover that your Sun sign (Aries, Taurus, Gemini etc.) is just the tip of the iceberg.

SUN SIGNS

Each chapter focuses on one of the 12 Sun signs of the zodiac. Your Sun sign is probably the area of astrology you're most familiar with, and is also known as your star sign, sign of the zodiac, or horoscope. Your Sun sign describes your core personality: the values and traits that stay true, whatever situation you're in. It's your default personality and it's hard to conceal. Even if you're not typical of your sign — for instance, a shy Leo or an extravagant Capricorn — your Sun sign's unique values always shine through.

♈ Aries	♉ Taurus	♊ Gemini	♋ Cancer
♌ Leo	♍ Virgo	♎ Libra	♏ Scorpio
♐ Sagittarius	♑ Capricorn	♒ Aquarius	♓ Pisces
♃ Jupiter	♂ Mars	☿ Mercury	♆ Neptune	♇ Pluto
♄ Saturn	☉ Sun	♅ Uranus	♀ Venus

YOUR FREE BIRTH CHART

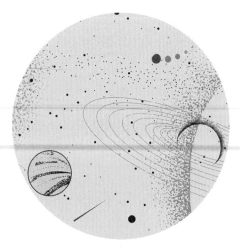

Visit: www.astro.com and click
the 'Free Horoscopes link, Charts
& Data, Chart Drawing, Ascendant'. Now
enter your birth information. If you don't
know what time you were born, put in 12.00pm. Your
Ascendant and the houses might not be exact, but
the planets will be in the correct zodiac signs and the
aspects will be accurate.

To find your Moon sign, look at the list of planets
in the grid on the left of your birth chart and you'll see
the first three letters of the zodiac sign the Moon was
in, next to it. You'll also discover the signs all your other
planets were in, which houses they occupied and the
aspect patterns they created at your birth.

THE SIGNS AND SYMBOLS IN YOUR BIRTH CHART

Each chart is a 360° circle divided into 12 segments known as the houses. The most important point in a birth chart is the Ascendant, sometimes known as your Rising sign. This is usually shown as 'AS' on the chart, and it shows the zodiac sign that was rising on the Eastern horizon at the moment you were born. It's always on the middle left of the chart on the dividing line of the first house — the house associated with the self, how you appear to others, and the lens through which you view the world.

BIRTH CHART INTERPRETATION BASICS

When you first explore your chart, you'll find that as well as a Sun and Moon sign you have a Mercury, Venus, Mars, Jupiter, Saturn, Neptune, Uranus and Pluto sign — and they all mean something different. Then there's astrological houses to consider, your ruling planets and Ascendant, aspects, and your element type. The art of astrology lies in synthesizing all this intriguing information to paint a picture of your, or someone else's, character, layer by layer.

Astrologers the world over have been studying their own birth charts, and those of people they know, their whole lives. And still they find something new in them every day. There are many schools of astrology and an inexhaustible list of tools and techniques, but here are the essentials to get you started...

PLANETARY ASPECTS

The aspects are geometric patterns formed by the planets and represent different types of energy. They are usually shown in two ways — in a separate grid or aspect grid, and as the criss-crossing lines on the chart itself. There are oodles of different aspect patterns, but to keep things simple we'll just be working with four: conjunctions, squares, oppositions and trines.

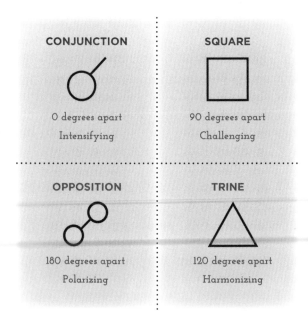

CONJUNCTION

0 degrees apart

Intensifying

SQUARE

90 degrees apart

Challenging

OPPOSITION

180 degrees apart

Polarizing

TRINE

120 degrees apart

Harmonizing

ZODIAC SIGNS AND RULING PLANETS

These are the keywords for the 12 zodiac signs and the planets associated with them, known as ruling planets. The planetary ruler of a person's Ascendant sign is always a key player in unlocking a birth chart.

Aries
(courageous, bold, aggressive, leading, impulsive)

Ruling planet Mars
shows where you act and how you channel your energy.

Taurus
(reliable, artistic, practical, stubborn, patient)

Ruling planet Venus
describes what you value and who and what you love.

Gemini
(clever, friendly, superficial, versatile)

Ruling planet Mercury
represents how your mind works and how you communicate.

Cancer
(emotional, nurturing, defensive, sensitive)

Ruling planet Moon
describes your emotional needs and how you wish to be nurtured.

Leo
(confident, radiant, proud, vain, generous)

Ruling planet Sun
describes your core personality and character.

Virgo
(analytical, organized, meticulous, thrifty)

Ruling planet Mercury
co-ruler of Gemini and Virgo.

Libra
(fair, indecisive, cooperative, diplomatic)

Ruling planet Venus
co-ruler of Taurus and Libra.

Scorpio
(regenerating, magnetic, obsessive, penetrating)

Ruling planet Pluto
deep transformation, endings and beginnings.

Sagittarius
(optimistic, visionary, expansive, blunt, generous)

Ruling planet Jupiter
travel, education and faith in a higher power.

Capricorn
(ambitious, responsible, cautious, conventional)

Ruling planet Saturn
your ambitions, work ethic and restrictions.

Aquarius
(unconventional, independent, erratic, unpredictable)

Ruling planet Uranus
where you rebel or innovate.

Pisces
(dreamy, chaotic, compassionate, imaginative, idealistic)

Ruling planet Neptune
your unconscious, and where you let things go.

THE ELEMENTS

Each zodiac sign belongs to one of the four elements: Earth, Air, Fire or Water, which share similar characteristics.

EARTH

Taurus Virgo Capricorn

Earth signs are practical, trustworthy, thorough and logical.

AIR

Gemini Libra Aquarius

Air signs are clever, flighty, intellectual and charming.

FIRE

Aries Leo Sagittarius

Fire signs are active, creative, warm, spontaneous innovators.

WATER

Cancer Scorpio Pisces

Water signs are sensitive, empathic, dramatic and caring.

THE 12 HOUSES

Birth charts are divided into 12 sections, known as houses, each linked to the 12 Sun signs, and are associated with different areas of life as follows:

1ST HOUSE
(associated with Aries)
Identity — how you appear to others and your initial response to challenges.

7TH HOUSE
(associated with Libra)
Relationships, partnerships, others and enemies.

2ND HOUSE
(associated with Taurus)
How you make and spend money, your talents, skills and how you value yourself.

8TH HOUSE
(associated with Scorpio)
Sex, death, transformation, wills and money you share with another.

3RD HOUSE
(associated with Gemini)
Siblings, neighbours, communication and short-distance travel.

9TH HOUSE
(associated with Sagittarius)
Travel, education, religious beliefs, faith and generosity.

4TH HOUSE
(associated with Cancer)
Home, family, your mother, roots and the past.

10TH HOUSE
(associated with Capricorn)
Career, father, ambitions, worldly success.

5TH HOUSE
(associated with Leo)
Love affairs, romance, creativity, gambling and children.

11TH HOUSE
(associated with Aquarius)
Friends, groups, ideals and social or political movements.

6TH HOUSE
(associated with Virgo)
Health, routines, organization and pets.

12TH HOUSE
(associated with Pisces)
Spirituality, the unconscious mind, dreams and karma.

ARIES
(21 MARCH — 20 APRIL)

Y ou are a passionate Fire sign ruled by action-oriented, take-no-prisoners Mars. Fire Sun signs are usually forthright, energetic and creative with an unrivalled lust for life. As the first sign of the zodiac, you are a natural leader, a pioneering go-getter who lets nothing get in your way. You like to be first and you play to win.

You accomplish your goals fast, fearlessly and furiously, and, yes, you may run out of steam a little towards the end of more complicated projects. But the momentum with which you propel everything you do is usually powerful enough to cover all the important stuff. Maybe let a more detail-oriented sign, like Virgo or Capricorn, tie up the loose ends.

LET'S GO!

You prefer acting rather than talking or thinking, and the more challenging a problem the higher its value seems to you. Your reactions are lightning fast, and you instinctively understand how to make things happen. This can make you a little impatient with more considerate types who like to weigh up pros and cons. Your natural assertiveness fires you up to get moving without delay — why would anyone want to waste time discussing the details? You have stuff to do and fun to be had!

You're not one to dwell in the past or overthink yourself into a corner. Leave all that introspection to the Water signs. You prefer to go it alone and act independently, as it means you don't have to wait about for anyone else. Besides, just one of you is quicker than any team of experts. The results may sometimes be a little rough around the edges — but the job gets done.

Your uncomplicated approach to life means you prefer to take things at face value, and if snags arise further down the line, you'll cross those bridges when you come to them. But instead what tends to happen is that you lose a bit of interest when you run into boring problems such as waiting for other people to make decisions, encountering funding issues or being told you're being unrealistic. When things slow down, you're often tempted to begin a new, exciting plan, which seems more fun... until you run into similar energy-sapping obstacles.

Give yourself time before you agree to something you won't really be able to give your full attention. The same can be said about your romantic relationships. Many Aries get married early in a flush of excitement, wishing they'd given things a bit more time at the start to make sure they were really compatible.

BRAVE HEART

Your courage is legendary, and that applies to matters of the heart as well as your physical prowess. You're not frightened to speak out about how you feel, and because you're more inclined to extrovert tendencies, you usually find it quite cathartic to express your emotions freely. You accept your feelings readily without prejudice or analysis — you feel what you feel — and that's all there is to it! As a Mars-ruled individual, anger can sometimes boil up to the surface, and you're no stranger to a good old-fashioned tantrum. But thanks to your emotional openness, your frustration tends to be explosive, short-lived and quickly forgotten. But explain that to the mild-mannered Piscean whose hair stood on end when you scolded them for not holding the elevator!

Where others fear to speak, you say exactly what's on your mind. You may have a reputation for being a little tactless or abrupt, but you're also admired for your wonderfully outspoken nature. You don't usually set out to intentionally offend anyone, but if you do say something out of turn, you'll not dwell on the consequences too much. More inward-looking Sun signs might gasp in awe at the apparent ease with which you brush off misunderstandings, but you don't place too much importance on chitchat. You say what most people are thinking, and secretly wish that everyone else would do the same. The world would certainly be a less complicated place if everyone were an Aries!

RAM OR SHEEP?

Your feisty bluntness can have other people thinking you're a tougher cookie than you are. But because you're so open and honest with others, you're genuinely stung when people you know well resort to underhanded or manipulative tactics to get back at you in some way.

It's not in you to be scheming or devious — you wear your heart on your sleeve. You yell, you stamp your feet — you may even stick pins in a few voodoo dolls, but then it's over. You worked through it. So discovering that other people have been plotting against you can come as quite a shock.

Handling other people's frustration and anger is certainly a life lesson you'll encounter — or will have now mastered. But you're hurt to the core if you discover you've been lied to. In a way you'd rather people just got plain angry or punched you, because then you'd know what you were dealing with. Honesty is your superpower, so to have it used against you can leave you feeling bewildered.

If wounded, you'll put on a brave face, but need plenty of alone time to piece yourself together. Unfortunately, not everyone is as confident in themselves as you are, so you may occasionally rub more introspective types up the wrong way. Luckily, though, you're not usually a brooder, and recover relatively quickly from any setbacks.

ARIES IN LOVE

You love with a childlike, uncomplicated joy. You don't have the patience for mind games and rarely waste time on somebody who cannot return your affections. You're open and honest about your feelings and not subtle, which can be a little unnerving! But your uncomplicated approach makes you a refreshing, exciting person to be in love with.

You can be a bit bossy at times, but your partner doesn't see this at first because they're so caught up in your ardent, blinding affection. You need a strong other half who can match your energy and won't be afraid of a challenge.

INSTANT ATTRACTION

You will have had more than your fair share of experiences of love at first sight; after all, you are the first sign of the zodiac, and first impressions mean a great deal to you. You fall hard and fast with a burning desire, and you're usually the one who initiates contact. You're not backwards in coming forwards and have a knack for knowing how to impress the person you have your heart set on. As you're not scared to approach people you like, you may have many love relationships in your life before settling on someone special. You have complete faith in yourself, but you take a while to feel that sure about anyone else.

As an energetic Fire sign, your sex appeal is obvious, though the intense heat can cool quickly if your lover has a lazy streak or seems to be a bit of a pushover. When you decide you really care about someone, you call off the attack dogs, and your chosen person will discover a very romantic soul that loves with the uncomplicated innocence of a child.

CARING — YES... SHARING — HMM

Even in your closest relationships you're an independent free spirit, so sharing your life with someone else can feel a little daunting. Cooking for another can feel like a big deal at first — never mind having to share your living space and time. But if your mate understands and is willing for you to take charge, there won't be too many shouting matches. Though if your partner begins to get too clingy you may have to have an adult conversation.

TRICKY EMOTIONS

You hate feeling vulnerable; only a few carefully chosen people ever really get to see the trusting little child in you. But when you feel safe and loved, you let your guard down completely. Your confidence in others' love is hard won, so if you feel taken for granted or disappointed in your partner, it can be devastating. A little naive sometimes, you can't imagine why your lover would be anything but honest and open with you at all times — manipulation just isn't your style.

If someone does break your heart, your grief is real and raw, but because you are able to express yourself so

Most Compatible Love Signs

ARIES You love a challenge, and only another Aries can handle your lava-hot passion without getting burned.

LEO You're both enthusiastic and energetic. Leos need to be admired, which you're happy to do — as long as they don't mind you bossing them around.

LIBRA You're not intimidated by anyone, but there's something mysterious and magnetically appealing about your opposite sign of Libra.

sincerely, you are able to process your emotions more quickly than the other zodiac signs. Phew!

WARRIOR SPIRIT

Ultimately, you are a fighter, and you won't give up on love because you know you deserve it and your self-belief demands it! You may experience your fair share of romances and breakups, but that's because you're a tougher cookie than most — the Universe knows you can handle it. You may have something of an epic frog-kissing journey to complete before finding your prince or princess, but where's the challenge in finding your true love straight away? You're not one to dwell on past hurts, and eventually see them

Least Compatible Love Signs

VIRGO Virgo won't make love until the house is tidy and they've watched the news.

TAURUS Dislikes being rushed and doesn't like being uncomfortable, which rules out your spontaneous desire to make love on the washing machine.

CANCER You just plain scare Cancerians, who need to feel safe, secure and well understood before anyone is allowed get close. You don't have time for that!

as milestones on the road as you battle your way to victory in love.

ARIES AT WORK

You love to lead, and you play to win — skills that can make you a legendary boss, and ultimately that's where you're heading! But to get the top-banana position you also need to master a few workplace habits and skills.

You tend to throw yourself into the deep end, or enthusiastically plunge into new projects without wasting time, which is all very commendable, and your boss will appreciate your energy. But a little more preparation will help when you get stuck or bored.

Be honest: you assume that thinking things through is just a delay tactic and that you'll fix any problems along the way. But a lack of foresight will cost you time, energy and probably money further down the line.

Learn some patience and impress everyone you're working with that you're not just a flash in the pan. Next time you have a great idea, think of what you are trying to achieve and how you will get there. Write up a plan of action, work out a budget and discuss it with people who know more about it than you do... they're thin on the ground, admittedly, but there must be someone!

WORK ON: TEAMWORK

Why do you have to work with others at all, darn it?! You can accomplish far more on your own... or so you think. And this may be true to an extent. But other people are a fact of life at work, and isolating yourself from them will probably just make you a bit unpopular, and more likely to be left out of the coffee round.

Let other colleagues know you're available and willing to contribute. See your work partners and teammates as a challenge to be mastered. Learn the art of compromise and discover how to work more flexibly. Nobody likes someone that pushes in and takes all the glory for themselves. Share your successes and include your colleagues in your thinking. Then when you do bump into an obstacle or have to deal with a difficult person, you won't be doing it all on your own.

Working in a group is a skill — and one that you'll have to get better at if you want to get to the top. But when your colleagues see how fast you learn and how willing you are to put yourself forward for challenging tasks, they'll admire your pluck, and will soon learn that you'll be an asset on their team.

You're a bright spark, but your super self-confidence can be a little overbearing. However, when your workmates see that you can also be trusted, they'll soon see your eagerness to please and impress as an asset.

TOP SKILLS

Your eagerness and boundless energy are admirable and will catch your boss's eye and keep you fresh in their mind. Not everyone is keen as you are to take on difficult challenges at work, and your innovative ideas will prove popular. You're never stuck for an answer and are often the one to kick off brainstorming sessions.

You're also a very quick learner, and absorb new information lighting fast. But sometimes it's wise to slow down a little. Make sure that your impatience isn't getting in the way of listening to what people want you to do.

When your employers trust that you will take on other people's opinions without argument, or can take criticism without stapling their tie to the desk, you'll be worth your weight in gold to any organization. And when you do get to the top, which is inevitable, you can be the one calling the shots — and everything will fall into its natural astrological order.

ARIES FRIENDS AND FAMILY

You're a fun and exciting friend with bags of energy. You're rarely still and, because you get bored easily, you usually have new hobbies and interests on the go. You prefer going out and doing something with your buddies rather than sitting around talking. Hot-air ballooning, watching motorcycle racing, zorbing and hiking might be stimulating activities for you, but not all your friends will be so active and energetic!

One of the things your friends love about you is that you stick up for them so readily.

You're fiercely protective of the people you care about, which makes for a formidable enemy. So woe betide anyone brave enough to annoy any of your friends — they'll have you to deal with. You love a good argument, though you prefer to call them 'heated discussions' when you're debating with pals. They, however, may see this differently!

You prefer to keep things lively in your social life, so you usually have a wide circle of people you see on a regular basis. Your warmth and enthusiasm attract people from all sorts of backgrounds. You enjoy variety, and although you're loyal to a handful of very close friends, you don't take offence when people disappear; you understand too well that life is like that. But you do get very hurt if a friend betrays or lies to you. Breaking your trust is agonizing for you because it's simply not in your character to treat people like that yourself.

Perfect Aries careers
- Lion tamer • Firefighter • Ambulance driver
- Professional athlete • Surgeon
- First-aid responder • Police officer • Soldier
- Pilot • Demolition expert

FAMILY DYNAMICS

You like your home life to be noisy, fun and adventurous. Camping trips, mountaineering, athletics and the gym are family favourites. You don't relish the cooking, cleaning and general upkeep of your home, but there's never a dull moment. Besides, who cares about the washing up when there's a cabaret happening in the lounge, a zoo in the kitchen and the family Olympic games in the garden?

ARIES PARENT

You're an encouraging, proud parent who gives their children plenty of room to grow. In many ways you're actually a big kid yourself, so you have a real affinity with the little ones and love their curiosity. You share their wonder and have a beguiling innocence that kids adore. You're the parent that doesn't mind if your kids get their hands dirty or have mismatched socks, and you actively encourage tree climbing, bug hotels and rough-and-tumble activities that daintier parents would shy away from. If somebody upsets your offspring, there's usually hell to pay — and you think nothing of telling teachers and other kids' parents exactly what you think of them.

ARIES CHILD

Aries children are fiercely independent, courageous and self-assertive. They learn early how to stick up for themselves and can sometimes be quite aggressive. Mars-ruled kids aren't particularly sulky, but they can have quite explosive tempers and they'll need plenty of exercise and activities to help them work through their high emotions. Aries kids can get fidgety if they're bored, and they can be super-competitive at games. If you want to entertain an Aries child, tell them they can't do something and watch while they prove you wrong!

HEALTHY ARIES

The creative power of the Sun has bestowed you with a robust constitution and athletic abilities. You excel at games and sport, and enjoy setting yourself goals and smashing through your targets. You're usually a fast mover, but are more of a sprinter than a long-distance runner. Your burn brightly but because you put so much energy in at the start, you can get exhausted. Ruled by energetic Mars, you put everything into your efforts but run out of patience if things get too samey. You like to change the scenery and to keep your goals interesting. Just changing your daily commute, or the grocery-store run, can give you a bit of a lift.

ACTIVITIES AND RELAXATION

Boxing, trampolining, hot yoga and running would all be excellent activities for your boisterous sign. You're no couch potato, and need to keep yourself busy. Netflix every night would have you, quite literally, climbing the walls.

You need space around you and plenty of fresh air — and you're not fussed if the weather is bad. Exercising in snow, wind and rain just adds to the challenge for you! You're not usually a team player, preferring the freedom of going it alone, but it's different if we're talking about sport. You excel at any physically demanding team sports and are usually a key player.

Most other zodiac signs just can't match you on physical prowess, and eventually even you can't sustain your cheetah-like pace indefinitely. Because you use up so much energy it's super-important that you match the energy out with energy back in and get plenty of sleep. You're more of a morning person than a night owl, and early nights will refresh your depleted batteries.

FOOD AND DRINK

You have a very healthy appetite and burn calories fast. As a Fire sign you enjoy hot, spicy food and are not a particularly fussy eater. Fast food works for you — as long as you balance it up with enough lively activity. If you could, you'd eat out at a different place every day. You don't always have the patience to cook, and the thought of sampling new cuisines is too tempting to miss out on. You're more of a street-food fan than a leisurely-candlelit-dinner person, and you prefer to grab and go and have a soft spot for food trucks and buffets.

Red meat, hot peppers and curries are Aries foods, and you have a penchant for energy drinks. You're not moved by bland tastes — the stronger the better you like it, but go easy on the caffeine and coffee. You, more than most, need to switch off before going to bed. Everyone should drink plenty of water, but you should really take this to heart as Fire signs tend to burn their liquids quicker than most, so don't get dehydrated!

Aries's preferred places
- Mountaintop • Racetrack • Bangkok
- Texas • Yellowstone National Park
- Sports stadium • Tent

TAURUS
(21 APRIL — 21 MAY)

You are a strong, silent, patient rock of a person — the metaphorical foundations on which the rest of the zodiac signs are built. As the second sign, you take what Aries initiated and you create something tangible, beautiful and enduring.

You are solid, trustworthy and unchanging, which can sound a little too sensible, but without your strength and dependability, everything else collapses. The salt of the earth, you work towards your goals slowly with determination.

Patience is your superpower. When you know something, somewhere or someone is right for you, you'll accept that it may take a long time to get there. But you know with some certainty that you will. You're not in a rush — you're suspicious of anything that's quickly won, believing the best things in life should be earned.

It's this intractable stubbornness that's so frustrating for the bubblier, quicker-moving zodiac signs hoping you might be a little more flexible.

When your mind is made up, you will not undo it, and if you suspect others of attempting to inveigle you, or they get pushy, you'll simply and calmly stop where you are and will not be moved.

You take such a long time to make careful decisions that, unless your chart has a hefty amount of Water, Fire or Air elements, you are extremely reluctant to back down. You quietly weigh up the pros and cons, often without discussing any problems with loved ones or hinting that you're mulling over a problem. The care and mental effort that go into your decisions usually mean your conclusions are fair and sensible. But, once in a while, your opinion may be questionable. This puts you in the awkward position of having to defend your position even when you know, at the back of your mind, it might not hold water.

VENUSIAN COWS AND RAGING BULLS

Taurus is ruled by delightful Venus, bestowing you with ample good looks and an easy charm. Even skinny Taurus have a solidness to their physiques, and they usually have well-defined eyes and curly hair. Exuding an inner confidence that can be quite irresistible, you long for a partner and will wait patiently for the perfect person. You don't usually choose to waste energy on chasing love — you attract it!

You conserve your physical and emotional energy, which on the surface may look like nothing ever bothers you. This can occasionally prove irresistible to some, who will amuse themselves by attempting to provoke a reaction in you. But you tend to carry on regardless, in your good-natured, peaceful way.

This often makes people wrongly think that you are an emotionless person or are not moved by others' trials and tribulations. Earth signs can get very emotional indeed; it just takes you longer to get there. You try not to be too pulled around by your feelings so that when you really need to, you can wield your emotional energy to awesome effect. You value your feelings very deeply and are not about to exhaust them if it's not necessary. If anyone has ever seen you truly lose your temper, they'll understand why.

At times you appear to tolerate the sort of bad behaviour in others that would have your friends running for the hills. That's partly because of your deep-rooted fear of change, where you might choose the devil you know, rather than risk plunging into the unknown.

But when your anger is aroused, it will evolve, almost imperceptibly, over a long time — sometimes over decades. Similar to the way water eventually carves a path through rock, once the trench is set, there's no going back. And, when you finally blow, it's usually life changing. When Bulls charge, they lose it; sometimes you might not even remember what happened. You see red and you become anger. This can be pretty devastating for the outwardly serene Bull. And it can take you a long time to recover.

All that emotion has to come out somewhere, which is also, incidentally, one of the reasons Taurus makes for a passionate lover. You will move mountains for the people you love.

WORK HARD — PLAY HARDER

You are a thorough and dedicated worker and you like to do things properly. If you have been pressured to take shortcuts in the past, you probably had a bad experience and won't get caught out again. People trust you to do a proper, honest job and you repay in kind whether you're a bus driver, sculptor, joiner, scaffolder or bank manager.

Taurus has a natural affinity with money, and a knack for accumulating plenty of it. You may own more than one business and your enduring personality gives you the perseverance and ambition to keep going even when times are hard. You trust that eventually you'll make it work.

You're certainly not one to venture your life's savings on a whim like other flashier signs of the zodiac. You invest your time and money in sensible businesses that will always be needed, such as farming, restaurants, property, gardening, banking and funeral services.

You're not a workaholic, Saturn-ruled Capricorn type who values work over leisure. Venus definitely has something to say about that. You work for money to buy you lots of lovely stuff! And you know how to enjoy a bit of down time. Sometimes people who don't know you mistakenly think you're lazy, but that's just because you know how to draw such a defining line between work and relaxation.

TAURUS IN LOVE

Your easy-going nature, down-to-earth sense of humour and Venusian good looks draw people to you. You don't fall in love easily, but when you do it's usually a life-long commitment as you are a faithful, loyal and devoted partner.

You're a great catch and bring a wealth of treasures to the relationship table, but you require your potential partner to tick quite a few boxes before you return their affections.

You have excellent taste and expect any suitors to be acquainted with the finer things in life. A traditionalist at heart, you respect the tried-and-tested, more conventional route to romance. You like being wined and dined. Candlelit dinners, flowers, couples' massages and cocktails at sunset all bring a rosy glow to your heart. But the person who is going to make the best impression also has to look, smell and sound good. You're a sensual creature, and a person's voice can be a deal-breaker for you — a melodious timbre in a sexy voice will have you weak at the knees. Good cooks definitely have a head start in the competition to catch your eye, as do bankers, jewellers, estate agents and CEOs.

HIDDEN PASSION

Venus, your ruling planet, blessed you with a dollop of loveable charm and serenity, so you won't have to work too hard to attract a suitable other half. When you sense someone is attracted to you, you'll play it safe and slow to begin with, choosing a steady pace that you feel comfortable with. Unless you have plenty of Fire and Air planets in your birth chart, you're not usually a spontaneous or overly reactive person, which might make it harder for potential mates to know if you are interested at all.

You don't give away your heart easily, or indulge in passionate affairs, but when you've made up your mind about love, you rarely let go. It may take you a long time to get excited about someone, but when you're sure it's a serious romance, you are one of the most passionate lovers in the zodiac — even giving sexy, intense Scorpio a run for their money!

EMOTIONAL SECURITY

You need to feel secure to feel safe, so commitment — whether that's discussing marriage, buying a house together or having a family — relaxes you, and makes you believe your partner is ready to settle down in the same way you are. You work hard for your rewards and are happy to share the spoils with the right person.

Taurus is a money-oriented sign, associated with the second house of the zodiac connected with earnings and possessions. And, rightly or wrongly, you often associate money with self-worth. That's why a joint bank account, with money coming in from both sides, is usually part of your romantic agreements. A healthy bank balance makes you feel secure and valued, so choosing someone whose financial intentions are similar to yours is imperative.

Once you're in a committed and secure loving relationship, you're a happy Bull. You shower your chosen one with affection and like to spend much of your time in their company, but this can be a little stifling for more freedom-loving partners. You like to have your loved ones close at hand, where you can see, touch and hear them. If they're not around you can get a little anxious.

Most compatible love signs

CAPRICORN Stable, traditional and sensible, you're both hard workers and have a mutual financial understanding.

CANCER This protective sign makes you feel safe and well looked after — and they're usually excellent cooks!

SCORPIO You're attracted to Scorpio's calm exterior and delighted by their secretly passionate interior.

Least compatible love signs

SAGITTARIUS Sagittarius might need a makeover, a shave, new clothes, a car and a home before being considered.

GEMINI You want absolute sincerity in a lover. To you, Gemini is all chat and no substance.

AQUARIUS You need a sensual, passionate lover. Aquarians just aren't.

It's only natural for the zodiac sign connected with money and possessions to be a little bit clingy with the most important thing in their lives. Once you are comfortable with someone, it's terribly hard to let go. So, when your other half gives you cause to feel insecure, or you fear they're spending more time with others (even the dog!), you can become jealous.

A Bull's jealousy is not subtle. You're not used to being rocked by your emotions — anyone who's seen you angry will testify to that! Strong feelings can cause extremes of behaviour in you. When upset, you're no stranger to taking a passive-aggressive silent stance and you may even attempt to control your partner.

It will take a few foot massages, expensive chocolates and declarations of absolute devotion, but when the dust settles and you feel reassured, your serenity and your faith in your partner will be restored.

TAURUS AT WORK

You're one of the most hard-working signs of the zodiac. If you make promises, they'll be delivered. You're not necessarily the speediest, but you take pride in your work, which is usually of excellent quality. Not a huge fan of change, Taurus is the sign most likely to have been in the same job for the longest time. Familiarity makes you feel more at ease, and when you relax you get comfy. You've probably had the same office chair for years or still drink from the same broken mug.

As an employee, you are productive, methodical and punctual, which doesn't sound that exciting, but it's music to your boss's ears. You are trusted to get on with the job without supervision and can be fully relied on not to steer away from the brief. You're not a multitasker, you are patient and calm and prefer to stick with one job until it's complete. There are surprisingly few people in the world with that skill!

STEADY AS SHE GOES

If you're at the helm, you run a steady ship where everyone knows the rules. You don't tolerate shoddy workmanship and you don't cut corners. You prefer the people you're in charge of to have been working with you for a long time. You can be a little uneasy with new faces, and a little suspicious of anyone who comes highly recommended, as you'll be the judge of that!

Employees need to prove their skills and earn your trust before you feel they're ready to take on added responsibility. As a reliable Earth sign, your workers know you're a safe pair of hands who is brilliant in a crisis. Once you trust someone you work with, you are extremely loyal and move mountains to help them if you feel they've been unfairly treated. There's nothing more stubborn than a Bull who's made up their mind!

YOU'RE WORTH IT

You have high standards but expect to be rewarded for your efforts. As the sign of the zodiac most associated with money, that's always going to be a key factor in any long-term position. You like to see definite rewards and to be given concrete goals to work towards. You probably prefer a regular, fixed salary rather than a performance-based percentage, not because you don't think you're up to it, but because you feel more secure with a predictable routine.

You find methodical and even repetitive work rather comforting. But that doesn't mean you're not creative. Ruled by artistic Venus, you're an extremely patient and artistic soul who can spend weeks perfecting a painting, working on a sculpture or composing a concerto. You're a comfort-loving creature who appreciates good workmanship and would make an excellent luxury clothes designer or furniture maker. You're also known for having the loveliest singing voice in the zodiac.

THERE SHE BLOWS!

You can probably count on one hand how many times you've really lost your temper in your life. You're extremely tolerant and hard to upset, but some people can take that as a challenge. Bulls aren't impulsive types, and can weather some really unpleasant situations for years. Your anger builds by tiny amounts, almost imperceptibly adding to the load. Then one day you see red. It could be a harmless little jibe or sarcastic remark that becomes the straw that breaks the camel's back — and all hell breaks loose. An angry Taurus is a force of nature. Any witnesses to

Perfect Taurus careers
- Banker • Farmer • Builder • Singer
- Gardener • Wine producer • Musician
- Sculptor • Interior designer
- Restaurant owner

your rage will never forget — or take you for granted again!

TAURUS FRIENDS AND FAMILY

As a Taurus you're probably the most loyal, steadfast friend in the zodiac. You're not the fastest to make new friends, being a little hesitant to trust new people. But once you've made up your mind about them, your companions can become lifelong allies.

You're the rock everybody needs in their life, and the people closest to you know you're the voice of reason in a crisis. When one of your herd is freaking out, you're the sensible person who sits them down, puts the kettle on and dishes out the comfort food. Sometimes friends just need someone to hear them, and you offer solace, a safe place to vent and wise advice.

FOOD AND MUSIC — TAURUS ESSENTIALS

Preferring when it's just you or a couple of old friends together, you're not a gregarious party animal. You have a calming, soothing nature and prefer a quiet night in instead of nightclubs and crowded, noisy bars. But you do love music, and concerts are a popular choice when you're feeling sociable — and if the gig involves food, even better. You take your food very seriously, and often meet friends or bond with new ones over meals, whether at a market, dining out or — your favourite — a home-cooked meal.

SWEET-TEMPERED

Unless you have a few Fire or Air sign placements in your birth chart, you'll be a patient friend, happy to sit in the doctor's waiting room with them or drive through traffic jams to help them get to an interview. You know that losing your temper just isn't worth your energy. Talking of anger, it's not that you don't get mad — far from it. But your friends may only have seen you really lose it once or twice at the most. You're a sweet-natured, calm individual, but if a friend takes advantage of your good nature once too often, you'll let them know in terms they won't be able to ignore!

FAMILY DYNAMICS

A stable, steady home environment is essential for your wellbeing. Ruled by Venus, you have refined tastes in home furnishings and your abode will be tastefully and comfortably kitted out. Your family kitchen is the heart of the home, and your children will be treated to home-cooked meals, at which you will excel. All Taurus love food, but quality is essential. Badly prepared or cheap fodder leaves you cold — in fact it can make you pretty angry.

TAURUS PARENT

Strong, reliable and patient, you are a tower of strength. You're always there to offer a broad shoulder to cry on. You don't usually get involved with rough-and-tumble playtimes, but your family appreciate that you are always there if you need them. You're not one for long talks about feelings or for getting over-emotional, but you don't need to be. Your family don't have to ask if you love them — it will be obvious.

TAURUS CHILD

Taurus children will do things at their own pace. If they suspect they're being rushed they'll dig in their heels and won't budge. Taurus often grow up with the same interests they had when they were young. Instead of getting bored, they seem to become even more enthusiastic and absorbed in their pastimes as they get older.

Painting, sewing, fishing and gardening can all end up being a lifetime fascination.

HEALTHY TAURUS

Robust, with a strong physique, you are usually in rude health. You're not terribly athletic but you do have plenty of stamina often brought on by sheer, dogged determination. When and if you do take up regular exercise, you prefer a predictable routine to fit into your well-ordered lifestyle. You like having a fitness buddy, but if they can't stick to the arranged times, you'll find someone who can.

A true Taurus is a slow, purposeful mover who has one speed — their own. You hate to be rushed into anything — even if food is on the agenda! If you're being harassed to get on with something, you'll simply stop in your tracks and close down. You win at life through force of will. You may be weathered, battered and bruised, but you'll make it to the finish line. Other zodiac signs just can't get anywhere near your pain threshold or match you on stubbornness.

FOOD AND DRINK

No sign of the zodiac is as enamoured with food as you are. For Taurus, food is an all-consuming experience. Food takes you to another world. Earth signs are attracted to tangible things, and eating involves all your senses — it's got to look as good as it tastes. But, of course, your passion for food can lead to overindulgence, which can cause weight gain. You're lucky that you have a sturdiness that doesn't look out of place on a person who's a few pounds overweight — you can definitely carry it off. And, traditionally, as a Venus-ruled sign, you're usually pretty easy on the eye, which can all disguise an extra bit of padding!

ACTIVITIES AND RELAXATION

Sensual, with exquisite taste in clothes, you spend good money on leisurewear. You're often the most stylish person at the gym or yoga class, wearing expensive, soft, natural fabrics. You're not quite as enamoured with exercise though. Getting sweaty, out of breath and uncomfortable with unkempt hair is all a bit too uncomfortable for you. You're not a Fire sign that needs to burn through excess energy or an Air sign that works out for their mental health. Earth signs prefer to conserve their energy.

The gym might not be your natural home, but enjoying being outside in the fresh air is a different story. You are a hardy walker, most at peace in the bucolic countryside with a lazy picnic on the agenda.

Taurus have turned lounging into an art form. Soft, deep chairs, flattering lighting, candles and soft music are basics in your home. Your bed will be unusually luxurious, with money splurged on sumptuous fabric. You are a real creature of habit, and a predictable bedtime is important. Taurus often can't sleep without being near an open window — even in the depths of winter.

Taurus's preferred places
- Luxury hotel • Lakeside villa • Vineyard tour
- Greek taverna • Music festival
- Cooking school • Country pub

GEMINI
(22 MAY — 21 JUNE)

Y ou are the most versatile sign of the zodiac. Intelligent, adaptable and effervescent, you're the cleverest — and most easily bored — kid in town. You're the third sign, ruled by inquisitive Mercury, the communications planet, and you know something about everything, but you're not much of a specialist. Once you get your mind around something new, you're already half-thinking about what's around the corner. Your puppy-like mental enthusiasm keeps you bright, boisterous and burning for more.

As the first of the zodiac Air signs, you view the world with childlike curiosity and your mind is rarely still.

Whether it's astrophysics or pottery, you have an unrelenting thirst for knowledge and new experiences. This butterfly mentality means you can sometimes struggle with the Earthlier qualities of stability, commitment and determination. You live so much in your mind that you might forget to return messages, turn up late for important events, and sometimes just stop halfway through sentences, chasing your own train of thought down a plughole. You can't imagine why anyone would mind that you missed the boat for a dinner date or would think it rude that you forgot to take your friend to a sports game. Maybe you were sidetracked by a phone conversation or suddenly had to understand how mathematical equations work... surely that's more important than being bang on time for your sister's wedding.

It's not that you're being deliberately scatty — you just get so engrossed with whatever has caught your curiosity (until you get bored) that the outside world ceases to exist.

Getting so easily abducted by your thoughts and ideas can make you appear disorganized to others — a bit flaky, even. But your agile wit and changeable personality mean there's never a dull moment when you're around. You have many friends from all kinds of backgrounds, but your airy, light-hearted demeanour can see you miss out on deeper, more fulfilling relationships.

DETACHED BUT KIND

Your emotional reactions are often as mysterious to you as they are to others. It's not that you don't have feelings — of course you do. It's just that you trust in more logical and intellectual pursuits. Strong emotion can feel disconcerting to you, and to lessen its pull, you may appear sunny and bubbly on the outside even if beneath the surface you're in a black mood.

Because you prefer learning about things rather than experiencing them, you often fool the people closest to you (and probably therapists everywhere) into thinking you are more in touch with the source of your emotional turmoil than you are.

WHICH TWIN TODAY?

It's the disconnect between your emotional and mental nature and your skill for impersonation that reflect the dual nature associated with your zodiac symbol, the Gemini Twins. You flit from funny, light and sociable to dark, indifferent and unfathomable. Your moods are as Airy and changeable as the weather, flitting from serene blue skies one minute to stormy rain clouds the next.

HUMOUR AND BOREDOM

Sensing your love of gossip and drawn in by your wicked sense of humour, people find you so disarming that they often overshare. Your flattering attention to detail and ability to mentally empathize let others feel they can let their guard down. They exchange more information than they intend, and hope you'll keep quiet.

You have probably learned the hard way to keep your mouth closed. Information and entertainment are your currency, and it's hard to resist not passing on some juicy gossip, even if it's with someone you shouldn't! It is quite possible for you to keep things to yourself, but if you're bored or restless the temptation may be just too strong. And a bored Gemini is dangerous.

You don't cope well with repetition or a predictable job. If you're uninterested, you'll procrastinate or scroll through social media until your eyes bleed. And when you're restless, you'll rock the boat just to see what happens. When boredom takes hold, your curiosity can bring out the 'dark twin', who can be provocative and manipulate facts for your own enjoyment. What you see as harmless banter might be unkind, wildly exaggerated or even blatantly untrue. This fickle behaviour can earn you a reputation as being superficial.

On the other hand, a focused Gemini is a genius at work. You shine when you're switched on mentally and are working in a job where no two days are the same. You are outgoing and sociable, with heaps of energy, and if you're involved in something exciting you can be an enthusiastic influence on others. When you're mentally engaged, you'll get through your work twice as fast as everyone else, and the results will be intelligent, thoughtful and entertaining.

You're most at home when you're learning and teaching. Gemini schoolteachers are an inspiration to their pupils because they feel such a clear affinity with the children's ever-changing and easily distracted mindset. You're also a whizz at puzzles and board games, and a master at general knowledge.

GEMINI IN LOVE

You're one of the friendliest signs of the zodiac, and you fall a little bit in love with anyone and everyone when you first get to know them. You're drawn to new people and situations in a way no other zodiac sign is. Where others are shy or even a little fearful of others, your boundaries are quite fluid.

You typically experience a few romances before you settle on one person. And Gemini is the most likely sign of the zodiac to consider an open or unconventional approach to relationships. You may prefer to live in separate houses or even in different countries. You're willing to consider love relationships with people much older or younger than you, and long-distance romances can work too, as long as you talk to each other regularly. You're attracted to people who are different to the norm, who are from a different culture or who live an alternative lifestyle. Open-mindedness and a willingness to try something different are Gemini aphrodisiacs. And — unless you have Earth or Water signs in your birth chart — you're unlikely to be the possessive or jealous type.

GEMINI TOGETHERNESS

For you to fall hard for someone, there must be something enduringly fascinating about your chosen person. A bright intellect and enthusiasm for life will keep you coming back for more, and sharing common interests will help you work towards a shared goal. A nimble dance partner with whom to master complicated steps will literally keep you on your toes — and any two-person sport, such as tennis, squash or snooker, will give you both an active focus. Games like backgammon, Trivial Pursuit and chess keep you challenging each other's mental skills, and if the pair of you can curl up together with a crossword puzzle, that's certainly a promising sign.

A compatible sense of humour is also essential. You'll feel oddly flat or bored with a lover who takes you too seriously. If your own stories, puns and witty remarks fall short, you might wonder what the point of the relationship is at all. Some light sarcasm and teasing will tickle your mind and keep the atmosphere light and airy.

Above all, you value open communication in your relationships. You love talking — it's your superpower! You need to feel your partner is on the same level and are only truly content when there is constant rapport.

TRICKY EMOTIONS

You either say 'I love you' all the time, to everyone and everything, or you voice it to a lover occasionally but only when you really, truly mean it. Falling for someone hook, line and sinker can take you by surprise. You're not wholly comfortable being so dependent on another person's affection. Because you're a little detached from your own feelings, experiencing such forceful emotions toward someone else can be unsettling.

You meet the world around you on an intellectual level, and living in your mind is your safe place. Romantic love brings overwhelming happiness and excitement, but it can also provoke tricky feelings like vulnerability or sadness when your other half has upset you. Jealousy and possessiveness are deep, strange waters for you — unmanned territory that can't be navigated by brain power or conversation alone.

TERRIBLE TWINS

You do your best to ignore your more disquieting emotions, but eventually those feelings will need to

Most compatible love signs

AQUARIUS You both have unusual and sometimes downright eccentric tastes, and never tire of each other.

PISCES You blend into one another seamlessly, not quite knowing where one ends and the other begins.

LEO You're a glamorous couple — you both enjoy being the centre of attention and you're attracted to Leo's outgoing, open nature.

Least compatible love signs

SCORPIO You're initially attracted to this mysterious zodiac sign, but all that brooding intensity terrifies you a little.

GEMINI You tickle each other mentally and you'll always be friends, but you'll drive each other a little mad in the long term.

TAURUS You're attracted by Taurus's smouldering, sexy aura but Bulls love routine and stability — values you're not that crazy about.

be experienced, and this disconnect can bring your broodier, moodier Twin to the table.

Analyzing and intellectualizing your emotions won't make them disappear, and experiencing an alien feeling like anger or fear, and not being able to think it away, can be bewildering. It's this dissociation that brings your dual nature to life. When you're unsure what's causing difficult feelings, your mood can quickly change.

Learning that you can be so affected by other people's emotions — and that your own actions have emotional consequences on others — will be your most transformative lesson. To bond with another, you must first bond with yourself — and once you recognize that, your relationships will go from strength to strength.

GEMINI AT WORK

As a flexible Air sign, you adapt very easily to new or changing situations. You're a quick, logical decision maker who instinctively knows what to do before the Earth and Water signs have had a chance to finish their first cup of coffee. You're an independent thinker but prefer to work in teams or with a partner because you need a constant flow of communication.

If you've been given a dull or repetitive task in a quiet office with nobody to talk to, you will quickly wilt. You're a restless soul when you're underemployed and may wear a hole in your desk from tapping your fingers or warp the floorboards from pacing up and down so much.

You have a brilliant mind, and it needs to be stimulated and exercised in your role. A job where you meet new people daily, or have changing surroundings, will suit you best. Preferring to be on the move in a job full of interesting challenges, you're not overly bothered about prestige or a high salary if it means you'll be stuck in a soul-crushing routine.

Your verbal dexterity and dazzling patter make you a gifted salesperson, convincing people they need things they're not even interested in. Your knack for understanding how other people tick is well suited to working in advertising, television, public relations and all communications industries.

POWERS OF PERSUASION

You're a friendly boss, always around for a chat and a catch-up. You're not interested in traditional ways of doing things, or how things may always have been done in the past. You want to try new methods all the time and you want everyone else to be as enthusiastic about it as you are! If you feel you're being held back, you'll talk your way around anyone who listens, and you can be deviously persuasive when you set your mind to it.

Embellishing facts to make your case more convincing, you're so plausible-sounding that you'll have yourself fooled too. Your mental flightiness allows you to see things from all sides, and even when the truth is staring you in the face, you can find a way to make it less 'real' and set in stone. It's this ability to make black white and white black that makes you such a brilliant salesperson, spin doctor or politician.

You're rather brilliant at translating complex ideas into workable plans of action. An excellent negotiator, lightning fast at working through new terms and conditions, you can see how to make things work instantly. But once conditions are agreed and actioned, you can lose interest — for you the absorbing, problem-solving, fun part is done.

A happy employee as long as you're always engaged, you'll likely be the chattiest person in the workplace. You enjoy interacting in large teams with a varied bunch of people. Talking on the phone is second nature, and jobs that entail constant interaction with people on the internet would also work out peachily.

Your naughty sense of humour guarantees people enjoy working with you and makes up for what you might lack in consistency. Often the one organizing the office party, you understand that when your workmates let their hair down, they share information that they probably shouldn't. If there's a secret, or a whiff of scandal, you'll either know all about it or have started the rumour in the first place!

UNPREDICTABLE AND MISCHIEVOUS

Gemini is the zodiac sign that's likely tried the most jobs. You'll probably have been keen to start young; you try your hand at a great variety of things before you settle on one type of employment. Even in later life you're more capable of changing your career than the other zodiac signs.

If you become bored at work, you'll be easily distracted and prone to mischief. Your 'other twin' will make an appearance and you may become disruptive or provocative just to rock the boat for your own amusement. Your unemployed mind will simply find something else to keep it occupied... gossiping with colleagues, scanning social media, learning the latest dance craze or Googling your colleagues to find salacious gossip will all fill the void. The greater the variety of jobs you try in your life, the quicker you'll learn which are likely to keep you motivated and entertained for more than a few months.

GEMINI FRIENDS AND FAMILY

Gemini is one of the most affable, sociable and outgoing signs of the zodiac. You adapt easily to what other people are doing and thinking, and you welcome friends from all sorts of backgrounds. Your eternal curiosity for novelty means you are especially attracted to people you don't know much about. You get obsessed about them for a while, and they'll feel flattered that you're so delighted to be in their company. But once you've gathered all you think you need to know, you hop along to the next exciting person. Old friends find your dilettante approach a bit grating, especially when they're pushed aside in favour of the new shiny person.

> **Perfect Gemini careers**
> • Advertising • Writer • Teacher
> • Translator • Gymnast
> • Computer programmer • Engineer
> • DJ • Juggler • Librarian

Your mercurial approach doesn't mean you're uninterested in other people's happiness or welfare. You're one of the most thoughtful people around and genuinely concerned with your nearest and dearest's happiness — and you're probably their go-to person when they need to put the world to rights!

Proximity to your friends matters because you value the communication so much and it's just easier to keep in touch with people you meet most often. Long-distance friendships might be hard to maintain for that reason.

You are particularly intrigued by people who may have alienated others because of their annoying or even disturbing behaviour. You, on the other hand, think it's their controversial credentials that make them so appealing! Spending time discovering why they're behaving that way, you want to get inside their thinking. But it's not always for the other person's benefit that you are so interested. You're not always looking to bond with people once you get under their skin; it's just your insatiable need to learn about the people on your path.

You're happiest when you have a large circle of acquaintances without having to get too involved with them on a more intimate level. You're not keen on getting sucked into any emotional dramas — you just want to have fun! You're an exciting, entertaining person to be around, wickedly funny and usually the centre of attention at parties. But you're not always the steady, reliable pal who'll be there through more emotionally draining times.

FAMILY DYNAMICS

Typical Gemini homes are not quiet places — they can be chaotic. You love gadgets and electronics: phones, games, laptops and televisions. Mercury-ruled people love puzzles, so in a Gemini abode there will always be a game of Scrabble, a crossword or a jigsaw in play. Your home doesn't have to be plush; it's more a base for when you come back from more exciting things elsewhere. It is typically modern, bright and stuffed with reading material; without a book, radio or television you'd be stuck for something to do. Your home is often the hub for other families and friends to congregate, and you like to keep an open-door policy. You're not too guarded about your space — the more the merrier!

GEMINI PARENT

You are naturally in tune with children's capacity for learning — and also share their low boredom threshold. You are uncannily youthful in that respect and are very much a team player with your kids. Sports and athletic clubs, scouting and dancing are all favourite activities — and you'll join in with as many of these as you can. You're never condescending, which means your children are usually your best friends. This is of course wonderful, but when it comes to structure or discipline, your authority isn't as well respected as you'd hope.

GEMINI CHILD

Gemini youngsters are amazing learners. It's essential that Gemini children learn to play by themselves because if they get bored, they'll make their own entertainment — and that's something you probably won't want to encourage! When Gemini children get emotional, they don't always understand what they need to make them feel better and can change character quickly. They're used to knowing the answer to everything, so this can be quite disconcerting. They may retreat into their own world while they figure things out, then emerge as their sunny, energetic, lively little selves once more.

HEALTHY GEMINI

As the zodiac's first Air sign, you need to move about. Air is never still, and you crave plenty of variety to keep you feeling active, positive and content. An unusually speedy walker, you often get to your destination faster than public transport.

Long hikes and planned tours aren't really your cup of tea, as you get a little impatient once you have the gist of things or can see the end point in the distance. By then, you're usually ready to take on the next challenge.

FOOD AND DRINK

Unless you have some Earth sign placements in your birth chart, eating the same food at the same time is not your bag. You tend to be more of a picker than a heavy-meal sort of person. In fact, you can find large plates of food quite off-putting. You prefer to eat little and often — much better to choose what takes your fancy from a buffet, or to satisfy your appetite by preparing yourself some small, interesting snacks.

New restaurants, cafés and market stalls are often just as interesting to you as the fare on offer. As food is such a vast subject for you to get your teeth into, you rarely tire of reading or hearing about it. Sometimes watching cooking programmes will satisfy your appetite almost as much as preparing the food itself.

You're a 'two-starters' type of diner rather than going for a large main course.

With a taste for the unusual, it's exotic flavours and new products that intrigue you. If someone offered you a peanut butter and artichoke sandwich, you wouldn't say no. You might not eat the whole thing, but you'll certainly give it a go!

Caffeine can send a restless Gemini into overdrive, so it's best to avoid coffee or energy drinks if you want a decent night's sleep. As you burn so much energy, you will need to keep yourself hydrated with plenty of water.

ACTIVITIES AND RELAXATION

Nimble and fast on your feet you burn more calories than the average person before you've set foot in a gym or added any extra activity to your normal day. You lose interest in repetitive training exercises, but Wii fit and interactive dance or Zoom lessons should be fun or entertaining enough to burn off some physical, and mental, steam. When you do need a workout, you tend to go for intense, short bursts of activity such as spin classes or interval training.

What you lack in strength and stamina you make up for in agility. If you have plenty of Gemini placements in your birth chart you won't necessarily have the strongest constitution, but your legendary flexibility can make you a spectacular gymnast. Yoga and dancing are also Gemini specialities!

Gemini's preferred places
- California • Wildlife safari
- Orient Express • Dubai • Pub/Bar
- Nightclub • Dance class • Foam party

CANCER
(22 JUNE — 22 JULY)

Ruled by the Moon, your ever-changing moods reflect the lunar cycles as they wax and wane. In astrology, the Moon represents our emotions, instincts and reactions, and with your Sun in the Moon's territory, your feelings are magnified. The Crab is your zodiac symbol, depicting your tough outer personality — protecting and hiding the softer, more vulnerable, inner you.

You appear well-organized and quietly confident, like the captain of a ship in charge of everyone on board. You don't need, or want, to be the centre of attention. You know what you're doing, and you're a private person who just wants to be left alone to get on with things. Your kindly, firm, maternal manner garners trust from the people around you, who instinctively understand that you're looking out for them and are happy for you to take control.

You can be a little shy, and even standoffish, with people you don't know, but that's just because you're such a giving person. People need to earn your trust before you reveal what a sensitive soul you are inside. It would drain your mental and emotional energy to invite just anyone under your shell. Over the years, the people closest to you appreciate that you take your time to break new ground, and they give you a bit more time and space to get used to new people and situations.

Your confidence in people has probably been hard won. From an early age, you may have been criticized for being oversensitive, too touchy or overreactive, and been told you need to 'toughen up' or 'live in the real world'. As a result, you built a shell, a protective wall, around your heart, which works well as a defence from an uncaring and unpredictable world. Like a lighthouse in a storm, you stand firm and strong in the toughest conditions. Your emotions may be in an eternal state of fluctuation and agitation, but your values, desires and ambitions remain unchanged.

TENACIOUS AND DEFENSIVE

When you set your heart or mind on something, you're impressively tenacious. You're not usually impulsive or forthright, preferring to wait and watch before deciding on a course of action. Like a crab under the cover of moonlight, you're too self-conscious to strut your stuff and launch yourself into the middle of the action. When you have your eyes on the prize, you're clever and focused, but rarely approach your goals directly.

A sidling, undercover advance keeps you hidden from danger, and then at the last moment, when the coast is clear, you'll raise your pincers, grab your treasure, then scuttle back to the safety of your home.

Once in your possession, you guard your treasures fiercely. The things that a true Cancer values most in life are home, family, food, money, old friends, memories and sentimental objects. You're not a feisty person generally, but threaten the things you care about and you'll get very defensive — even a little aggressive — in your desire to keep hold of the things that matter.

LETTING GO

One of your greatest life lessons is to let go of past hurts. This is particularly hard for you to do because your memory is so incredibly good. You, more than any other sign, have detailed memories from childhood of people, pets and events that others have long forgotten. But clinging to old ideas of yourself, or not forgiving people who let go of you, stops you from evolving and venturing forward into the world... but the world really needs you!

CARING AND CATASTROPHIZING

Whether you're male or female, the Moon is linked with motherhood, and you are a born caregiver. Your instincts are to love, nurture and protect without asking for much in return. You're a tough nut to crack, because inside you're the softest, most beautiful soul, sensitive and easily hurt. Once you care, and let people into your enormous heart, you don't quite know how to give them up.

You love nothing better than a bit of catastrophizing, because it confirms your fears that everything is about to go terribly wrong. You're the person who brings

up that one time when things did go badly in the past
— and your memory of it is crystal clear, even if you
weren't actually there! You're no stranger to a bit of
overdramatizing for effect, and you feel it's your duty to
help other people prepare for inevitable calamities.

When things go awry for people you love, you're
genuinely sympathetic. Their pain and disappointment
chimes with your own vulnerabilities, and you're a
wonderful listener. Never judgemental or harsh, you
don't question much about what happened; someone
you love is in trouble — that's enough. You'll offer the
coat off your back, a warm, safe place to spend a few
nights, and a nourishing meal. It won't even enter your
mind that you may be inconvenienced or out of pocket
for a while. The people you love come first. End of story.

LAUGHING TILL YOU CRY

All Cancer people are capable of a little lunar madness
and, especially when younger, you'll be a slave to your
constantly wavering inner landscape. Absorbing the
moods of others, you know how they're feeling, perhaps
even before they do.

You will no doubt have learned that other people
don't always mean to hurt you with their thoughtless
comments or insensitive actions.

Most people are nowhere near as tuned in to the
world of feelings as you, and would be mortified to
think you'd taken offence. They're genuinely confused
by your hurt reactions, baffled you could take such a

trivial thing to heart. If you're really hurt by someone's behaviour, you retreat into your shell; the silent treatment usually gets your message across. But if a loved one has angered you, it's a different story. It happens rarely, but when you take revenge it's usually in secret, quietly executed and devastating!

Thank goodness you have an excellent sense of humour to take the sting out of the most emotionally tense situations. Laughing reminds you that nothing is ever that bad — even if it feels really intense. You love it when beloved friends have the nerve to poke fun at you, because you know there is no malice intended.

CANCER IN LOVE

When you're attracted to someone, it scares you a little. Your first instinct is to hide and think it through, which usually means worrying about how things could pan out. After all, it could all go miserably wrong... like that time you were hurt in the past... or when your friend's husband was caught cheating. Your mind spins out before you know any real facts about your sexy stranger.

Training your imagination will probably turn out to be a lifetime's endeavour, and you have such a tender heart that romance may be something of a learning process. As you get older and better understand your own and others' requirements in relationships, you'll learn to be more realistic. But you, more than any other zodiac sign, have the emotional capacity and understanding to navigate the human heart.

GIVING YOURSELF AWAY

When someone intriguing takes the first steps to get to know you, it can set off your defence mechanisms, and you'll be wary. Secretly you'll be flattered, but you'll worry yourself into a frenzy. And all this happens before you even know if this person is even truly flirting with you. You understand what a big deal giving even a tiny piece of your heart is — because the rest of your heart is usually close behind.

When you've been reassured enough from a potential lover, or have decided to trust him or her anyway, you are one of the most romantic people in the zodiac. You're an imaginative and generous lover, and you'll place your partner at the centre of your universe.

COME INSIDE MY SHELL

When you choose to love somebody, you're all in. When you let someone inside that crabby shell, there's no half measures. Domestic bliss is your aim, and setting up a home and family will be paramount. Whether you're angling for a big house full of children or are happy with a pretty little garden and a budgie, your home setup is where you feel safe, secure and loved.

You put down roots when you're at home, intending to build a base for life — and your partner needs to share that vision. Fire and Air signs may be too independent and adventurous for you to settle down with, or you'll need to make sure you both have a clear understanding of what the other needs. As long as the trust is there, you can be happy with someone who wants space to do their own thing.

Emotional compatibility is the single most important factor in your relationships. Your bond with a lover is so tight that you'll feel it if something isn't right — and will be hurt or confused if they're not sharing every emotion with you. You expect to be able to talk to your other half about everything — and expect the same level of openness from him or her. You make it so easy for others to express themselves that this isn't usually a problem. And when you have a contented, established relationship with a happy home life, you'll love without asking for much in return.

Most compatible love signs

TAURUS You both crave security, loyalty and a healthy bank balance — and you'll adore each other's sensual nature, too.

CAPRICORN Your opposite sign is patient and reassuring, and can teach you how to balance home and career.

SCORPIO You understand Scorpios because you are both emotionally driven with cool exteriors — they'll be tolerant of your changeable moods.

TRICKY EMOTIONS

When your emotional needs are met, you tend to place your partner on a pedestal. You will defend their actions, and sometimes excuse them, even when friends or family might raise an eyebrow. It can take a lot of talking you around to see that your loved ones are anything but perfect.

When you do have a disagreement with your partner, things can get heated fast, and the insecurity can knock you off balance. Your fight-or-flight response is strong, and disagreements or misunderstandings can fill you with foreboding. Your beloved may accuse you of being overly dramatic, or too needy, and that can wound you. It's difficult for you to remember that all relationships have to navigate

Least compatible love signs

AQUARIUS You want someone to build a comfortable home with, but Aquarius has plans to join the circus.

SAGITTARIUS Sagittarius are warm-hearted and enthusiastic, but tactless. You need someone to be your soulmate, not your puppy.

LIBRA They say all the right things, but do they feel them?

a few hurdles from time to time, without causing insurmountable problems.

Even when there's nothing to worry about, your oversensitive nervous system may pick up on others' energies and you'll be tempted to interpret them to suit your own suspicions. This can leave your partner feeling perplexed. It may take a while for your defences to come down again, but when they do, you'll be back to being one of the most generous and loving souls in the zodiac.

CANCER AT WORK

Your ideal work situation involves looking after people to some degree. One-to-one employment on a personal basis such as a healthcare professional, counsellor or beauty therapist fulfils your selfless enjoyment of making other people happy. But your understated, excellent people skills also mean you would excel as a charity CEO, a public-relations consultant or a politician campaigning for better conditions in your community.

You also love working with food — it's your way of nurturing people, and it's not an accident that you're known as the best cook in the zodiac. Working as a chef or in the catering industry would suit you well with your caretaking, comforting abilities. In an office, you often assume the role of the mother or father figure, lending a sympathetic ear and making sure everyone is happy, comfortable and listened to.

You're that popular work-auntie who spoils your colleagues with fabulous homemade cakes, or assumes the protective father figure — the union rep or person who sits on the staff council.

Your discretion and good judgment will be an asset whether you are an office manager or an HR director. And your commitment to solving problems, and attention to detail, ensure that you'd be an impressive project manager.

Wherever you work with other people, your instincts are to protect and encourage them, whether they're children, elderly people or plants! Cancer is as green-fingered as Taurus when it comes to gardening. Working as a farmer, professional gardener or brewer would also satisfy your instinct to nurture, cultivate and nourish.

HOME SECURITY

Like Taurus, you prefer a regular salary. You're better with money than most, appreciating its security. You're a saver at heart, and even when you're pretty flush by anyone else's standards you're likely to plead poverty. The thought of not being able to pay your rent or mortgage, or risking your home, is one of your biggest anxieties, and you're not frightened of taking on jobs that others would turn their noses up at to keep a roof over your head.

If you're in charge of putting food on the table at home, you'll clean streets, unblock toilets or busk outside the train station in the pouring rain if it brings in enough cash to care for your children. It's this dedication to others that also causes you to be a passionate fundraiser or advocate for people less fortunate than yourself.

If you're looking for work, you'll usually find it. In your quietly tenacious way, you'll prove yourself invaluable. You're stealthily ambitious and determined to keep your position for as long as possible. Your people-handling skills and unassuming manner impress most employers, who will appreciate your loyalty and calm manner.

Freelance work or self-employment is fine as long as you're watching your bank balance rise steadily. But if the cash flow runs low, or you're living on credit cards, you'll be an unhappy Crab!

CRABBY BOSS

Behind your shy exterior beats the heart of a leader! As a gentle but firm parental figure, you often rise to the top of your profession. Co-workers admire your quiet, strong leadership skills and learn that a little cajoling and kindness from you is sometimes all that's needed to exert authority. You're not a demanding or aggressive boss, preferring to connect with your work buddies on a more personal level.

Your colleagues feel comfortable with you and appreciate that you're sympathetic to their family needs. You'll pick up any vibes if things are off-kilter and understand what's needed to resolve any conflict. You care, but you will also demand loyalty.

If an employee, or a member of your team, decides to leave, you can't help but take it a little personally. It can feel like someone in your family is rebelling against you or has outgrown the nest. When workplace relationships feel strained, you worry. And a stressed-out Crab will go inside their shell if they feel they're being attacked — even if that's just in their imagination!

CANCER FRIENDS AND FAMILY

Everyone needs a Cancer friend. You are a loyal, caring, funny companion, and you know how to keep a secret! Unless you have Fire or Air in your birth chart, you can be a little shy when meeting new people. But when you do make a friend, you're usually buddies for life. You're the best listener, and you offer support where you can. Even with long-distance friendships, as soon as you get together again, you slot back like peas in a pod, as though you've never been apart.

Old friends know how to calm you down if you've been worrying or overanalyzing. They're used to you dramatizing your woes, and know you just need to vent your concerns. After a sympathetic ear and a few glasses of wine, you feel reassured that the world is a safe place.

NO PLACE LIKE HOME

You're not quite happy without a hearth to call your own. Your home is your sanctuary, a safe, secure place where you come out of your shell, relax and enjoy your family. Home furnishings will be comfortable and perhaps a little weather-worn by children and pets over the years. You're sentimental about old things with personal memories attached, which can mean you end up keeping objects well after their use-by date.

Food is your comfort and your passion. A superb home cook, you usually spoil your family with culinary delights. Or, if you're not into cooking, you'll almost certainly stuff your cupboards with quality goodies. Always finding excuses to stuff loved ones with food when visitors come to call, you'll set aside plenty of tasty morsels for everyone. Wasting food is a terrible crime in your eyes, and if you can't feed it to family, friends or pets, you compost it or keep it for your wormery.

HOARDING, OR BUILDING A SHELL?

You have a passion for collecting things, especially antiques or items of sentimental value. The most likely sign of the zodiac to hoard, once you have something in your home, it's difficult to let it go. Your possessions may eventually even feel like they're part of your shell, a wall you build around yourself, and everything dear to you.

If you feel insecure, you worry, and when you're anxious, you cling to the things you love. The most prepared person for a worst-case scenario, you probably have a fully kitted-out nuclear bunker or a shed full of tinned foods and bottled water. Your

> ### Cancer preferred places
> • Your own home • Traditional seaside
> • Moonlit cruise • Lake District
> • Canal boat • Meditation retreat
> • Cosy cottage • Food festival

house is packed to the gunnels with emergency supplies, usually including out-of-date medicines, batteries and Wellington boots with holes.

CANCER PARENT

Born to nurture, care and protect, you are the zodiac's most dedicated parent. You love to share your vivid imagination with your children. A wonderful storyteller and inventive game player, you understand the inner workings of your child's mind. The embodiment of tenderness and patience, you never tire of your children's demands on your time.

CANCER CHILD

Super-sensitive and prone to quick changes in mood, lunar-ruled babies often pick up on the energies around them without realizing that's what they're doing. Once reassured by their parents, they feel safe and secure again, eager to learn and play. They're extremely curious but can get overwhelmed in chaotic, noisy situations. These creative little souls prefer making cakes, drawing and playing at dress-up to rough-and-tumble adventures.

HEALTHY CANCER

You're sensitive to the phases of the Moon, which push and pull your emotional states. Your fluctuating feelings are the main gauge of your wellbeing. When you're feeling happy, safe and secure, you have heaps of energy, a hearty appetite, and all feels well with the world. When your feelings are out of whack, your sensitive digestive system can be the first to feel something's not right.

Sometimes at a full Moon you need to be a little kinder to yourself, as you can be your own worst critic when you're feeling out of sorts emotionally. This state of flux can be reflected in worry or stress in your body. No other sign is as affected by their own positive or negative thoughts and emotional states. If you are prone to feeling unwell when anxious, the same should be true when you're feeling strong, and therefore able to heal yourself.

ACTIVITIES AND RELAXATION

You dislike feeling uncomfortable, so getting sweaty and breathless isn't your thing — and aggressive forms of exercise disturb your equilibrium. Gentler forms of physical action, such as yoga, walking, dancing and swimming, soothe your nerves and help you coordinate your physical and emotional energies.

Being near water relaxes you almost as much as swimming in it. A walk along a beach or a stroll by a river soothes your water-ruled constitution in a magical manner. You're a sensual person, and the gentle rhythm of the waves just feels right on a very primal level.

FOOD AND DRINK

For better or worse, food is usually your chosen comfort. You tend to eat when you're feeling anxious, bored or excited, and sometimes just because it's delicious and wonderful! You love traditional, old restaurants steeped in history almost as much as you adore a home-cooked roast dinner with friends at home.

For you, food is best as a family affair, and you don't need much of an excuse to prepare an elaborate meal or mouthwatering cake for a birthday or special occasion.

Cooking and sampling your delicious meals can cause unwanted weight to creep up on you. But your talents in the kitchen mean you're flexible and willing to experiment, so it shouldn't be too much of a chore to choose lighter or more unusual options.

As a Water sign, drinking plenty of fluids keeps you feeling balanced. A glass of delicious wine or an exciting cocktail will often be chosen as a special treat. If you punish yourself for eating and drinking too much, you can become entrenched in some unhealthy habits, or be subconsciously sending yourself unhelpful messages around food. 'A little bit of what you fancy does you good' would be a healthy motto.

Perfect Cancer careers
• Nurse • Nursery teacher
• Social services • Relationship counsellor
• Insurance • Gardener • Midwife
• Museum worker • Chef • Security guard

LEO
(23 JULY — 23 AUGUST)

Y ou are a regal, dignified, courageous Leo, ruled by the life-giving creative force of the Sun. And like the Sun, your place is at the centre of the solar system, where everything revolves around you!

In a birth chart, the Sun represents the self, the ego, the personal spark of the divine, which means you need to shine. With your passionate, creative, Fire sign energy, you're full of warmth and positivity — and you sparkle with life.

Commanding and authoritative, you can have a slightly condescending manner, but that's usually because you genuinely feel you know what's best for everyone. You were born to lead the pack, to encourage, protect and provide for others — so you need other people to give you a sense of purpose. Your motivation is usually to make other people happy and, yes, you can be a little bit firm in enforcing your rules sometimes. But you know you are strong and brave, and that your intentions come from the heart. It's this generosity of spirit that makes you one of the most popular signs of the zodiac.

You're a true people person and you enjoy nothing more than basking in the love you feel for others. This is one of the reasons you are attracted to the spotlight so much. Love is your reason for living. When you're the centre of attention, or on stage in some way, the applause and validation fill you with rays of joy, which you radiate back out to your admirers like a little Sun.

BOSSY OR JUST RIGHT?

You're an enterprising, vigorous worker who appreciates that you must put in the effort to be able to afford the good things in life. Whatever your job, you tackle it with intensity and determination and expect to be well-rewarded. You are one of the zodiac's most lavish spenders, with a penchant for luxury goods. A healthy work ethic is essential if you're to keep up with your swanky tastes and social life!

When you get your teeth into something, you're dynamic, focused and completely absorbed. You'll be directing other people, coming up with brilliant ideas and generally working yourself and everyone around you very hard.

As you are so well organized yourself, it's difficult for you to watch other people live more chaotic, less structured lives. You only want the best for your loved ones, and you're so confident and self-assured that it's very hard to resist not intervening when you think they're making a mistake.

You often find it easier to get others' lives in order, rather than concentrating on your own priorities. This is partly because it's easier for you to focus on what other people need out of a genuine concern for their welfare. But it's also because you're such a naturally extroverted character that doing things for yourself, on your own, just doesn't excite you that much.

Some of your friends and family may label this overeagerness to help as bossiness. But you'll usually argue that you're just pushing them to be the best they can — and ignore their pleas! The thing is, Leo, you're such a wise and knowledgeable person that others will naturally gravitate towards you for advice anyway. So if you do give people some space, they'll probably feel a little anxious that you're not going to hold their hand, and will come running back for help.

LEO TIME

It's a Leo myth that you're a 'lazy lion'. You're one of the zodiac's most dedicated workers, but once the graft is done, you play, luxuriate and indulge your senses. You're an exuberant partier with exquisite tastes. Champagne bubble baths, expensive nightclubs, the finest wines known to humanity, clothes of spun gold... male or female, you embody the playboy archetype.

You're actually no lazier than anyone else, but because you expend so much energy working and playing, you do tend to sleep more than most. You love a lie-in and certainly enjoy being catered for. You will put in extra hours at the office if it means avoiding menial chores. No self-respecting true Leo will look you in the eye while pulling hairs from the plughole. You'll happily hire nannies, dog walkers, cleaners, accountants and sometimes chefs to free up your precious time, leaving you to enjoy your hard-earned Leo time.

DON'T IGNORE ME!

The problem with thinking the world revolves around you is that when there's nobody around to watch you be fabulous, you might as well be invisible. Nothing hurts you more than being ignored; after all, you're doing 'all this' for everyone else's benefit. But it's not just that the attention isn't on you; it's more that when there's nobody else around, you're forced to focus on yourself. You're not one for self-contemplation, but that's exactly what you need from time to time because you could do with balancing out your need for external validation with some of your own healthy esteem. You must have time out from others to remember what you want.

You have a large number of acquaintances, some of whom don't really know the real you — and you don't want to be one of them! Deep down you might be a little scared or insecure that you can't or don't actually live up to your extraordinary reputation. You can be all bluff and bluster, and you secretly fear that your roar is more impressive than your bite. When you do willingly spend some time on your own, you might be pleasantly surprised.

Take a night off and see what happens — just you, no social media and no communication with the outside world. Find out who you really are, Leo. It won't take long for your creative instinct to kick in and you'll find that making something will give you a purpose, without requiring an audience. Dressmaking, painting, collage and baking are projects where you can share your creations with the people you love — and they'll really appreciate your generosity.

You don't often let other people see you when you're not 'on show'. You're all for false eyelashes, high fashion, sharp suits and flash cars. Your loved ones will see past your glam-armour, but perhaps you need to be a little kinder to the raw, unshaven, dressing-gown-and-slippers you, too. Deep down you're actually just a little pussycat asking to be loved.

LEO IN LOVE

Love is your language, Leo. As an exuberant, warm, effusive person you don't find it difficult to show your affections. You feel alive when you're attracted to someone new — full of possibilities and puppy-like enthusiasm. You're an excellent judge of character and will normally be pretty sure that your intended will at least feel some of the excitement you're experiencing. If you're not quite sure, you will need encouragement... you're not going to make a fool of yourself for someone who's unable to return your affections.

You'll be tentative at first, and if there's any uncertainty you'll hold back until you're sure you can win his or her heart. The slightest hint of reciprocation will light the touch-paper, and then you'll gleefully pounce. You're all in for love. You don't understand why anyone would play mind games — if you're both sure of one another, there's no point in pretending otherwise. More fearful or cautious zodiac signs may try to play it cool with a new lover, as they build up confidence, but when you get the green light you want the whole world to know how happy you are.

Grand romantic gestures don't get more dramatic than a Leo in love. You take all the conventional love clichés and cover them in gold and glitter. You love like you want to be loved in return — with an adoring, ardent, unquenchable passion. Thinking you can show how much you love someone by showering them with gifts and attention, your other half will be bowled over by your generosity and care — and perhaps a little overwhelmed.

When you put so much of yourself into making your life together a fabulous romantic adventure, you do expect your partner to reciprocate in kind. The problem here is that few people find it so natural and easy to be as generous with themselves as you. You set the bar so high that it's a lot for your lover to live up to. They might be worried about spending too much money on lavish gifts, or a little timid in expressing so much emotion.

This can be disappointing for Leo, as you crave public shows of affection. If someone loves you, they too should trumpet it from the heavens, empty their bank account and plan oodles of secret romantic trips, because that's how you do it — that's how love is done! You can be a hard act to follow for more modest or timid types who show their affections in a quieter, less dramatic way. And you have to learn that love can be deep and passionate without everything being for show.

PLAY TOGETHER, STAY TOGETHER

Togetherness is hugely important for you in a relationship. You can accept if your other half has other obligations and responsibilities, as long as your time together is spent doing something interesting. Shared pastimes are vital, so finding someone with a matched love for drama and entertainment would be a big plus. Getting excited about the same things — whether that's frequent trips to the movies, attending dance classes or a love of cosplay — will fuel your need for fun and togetherness.

After the passion cools to a steadier sizzle, you'll be concerned if your lover is happy to sit at home watching Netflix every night. You want to be seen and heard, preferably dressed to the nines at a millionaire's yacht party or an exclusive casino! Your beloved will hopefully enjoy being part of a fashionable or exciting social scene, because if they're happy to lounge around in an old tracksuit covered in dog hair, you may have to rethink how you're going to make things work.

TRICKY EMOTIONS

What other people think of your partner is a big issue. If friends or family disapprove, you'll do your best to win them over by overemphasizing their good points or making them out to be more glamorous or exciting than they actually are — or want to be. This tendency to gloss over or embellish the more mundane aspects of your life together can make your partner feel that they're not living up to your expectations — or being allowed to be who they are.

You are extremely proud of your partner and want to show him or her off — and you see their behaviour and appearance as inextricably linked to your own personality. So when your adored chooses to be themselves, happy to spend all day reading or tinkering

Most compatible love signs

LIBRA What a glamorous, charming pair — you both know how to impress other people and love being the centre of attention.

SAGITTARIUS You're the two most generous people in the zodiac. You'll have heaps of fun and enjoy emptying your joint bank account together!

GEMINI The sparkling entertainment team is here, and neither of you will get a wink of sleep when the other is around.

with their car, you can feel ignored and alone — two emotions you're uncomfortable with.

You are loving, supportive and generous in your relationships but you probably need to learn that being alone together and making each other happy is more important than the drama you play out for your adoring public. When you develop your own self-worth and realize that no other person defines you, you'll grow more accepting of your other half and less defined by what you imagine everyone else is thinking.

LEO AT WORK

On a deep level you respect that if you are to enjoy the best things in life, you need to work solidly for them. Your perfect job is one where you can shine and

Least compatible love signs

LEO You can get jealous when there's another big cat on the scene, stealing all the limelight.

SCORPIO Lots of passion initially, but Scorpio's broody emotions and shady game-playing are too underhand for an upfront Leo.

CAPRICORN Goat people are not usually emotionally demonstrative, which will cool your need for praise super-fast.

be admired while making oodles of cash. You want
to bring people joy and pleasure, and to be heartily
rewarded and thanked for your efforts. You sometimes
have so much fun at work that it can appear that
you're not stressed out or worried enough to be
doing it right. But you rival Virgo for being the most
organized sign of the zodiac.

You are reliable, responsible and loyal, and have
a natural ability to take control of any situation. Your
healthy self-esteem commands your colleagues'
respect. You'll have your eye on the top job, but you
need to watch that your ego doesn't rub co-workers
the wrong way. Your desire for attention and praise can
mean you need to remember to let more unassuming
personalities have their time in the spotlight.

LOOK WHAT I DID!

As one of the most creative and artistic signs of the
zodiac, finding work that's an extension of your self-
expression would be an ideal fit. Whether you are
offering gorgeous artwork, cooking wonderful food or
crafting unique furniture, you need to be proud of your
accomplishments and feel that they enhance other
people's lives too.

You are happiest in a position where you can stand
by your work and proudly declare, 'I did that!'

Working in a job where there are not many
opportunities to shine or progress wilts you and
undermines your self-confidence. You actually need a

good deal of encouragement, especially when you're in a new position. You thrive when you have an audience, so working on your own or behind the scenes is not ideal... unless there's a regular award or prize on offer for your achievements.

WELL DONE, LEO

You excel in any position where the focus is on you. Acting is often described as the perfect job for Leo because it involves performing in the spotlight, receiving applause and adopting a glamorous public image. The entertainment industry has a magnetic pull for Leos looking for the limelight, and singing, dancing or a career in music will be high on your list.

You love a touch of drama, so you excel in careers that allow your daring, extroverted nature to roam free. But even in less glam industries, when you're excited about what you're doing you'll enthusiastically extol the virtues of your wonderful project, exclusive shop, exciting department or unbeatable team.

People who are wise to your susceptibility to flattery can take advantage a little. For example, you may be pleased to accept an extravagant job title in place of a pay hike or be credited for something that doesn't matter in the grand scheme of things. Flashy diversion tactics may distract you for a while, but you're no fool. You always had your eyes on the top job — and that's naturally where you're headed.

KING OF THE JUNGLE

Leo takes charge instinctively, so being where the buck stops is where you are most comfortable. Magnanimous or tyrannical, there'll be no mistaking who's in charge. You're a fearless decision maker, calm in a crisis — and the people working for you respect and trust your judgment.

Your love of showing people what to do and encouraging them to grow makes you a popular boss. A patient teacher, you want others to appreciate your wisdom and experience, and to show some gratitude for your efforts. In return, you are generous and reward loyalty handsomely. It's Champagne all round when you're celebrating success, and you thoroughly enjoy watching people bask in the benefits you provide as the leader of the pack. Acutely aware of the need for downtime, you're happy to see your employees let their hair down when they've been working hard. You're the kind of boss who, as long as nobody questions your authority, is happy to let your team finish early on a Friday.

Perfect Leo careers
- Actor • Influencer • Fashion designer
- Circus ringmaster • Opera singer
- Cruise-ship entertainer
- Comedian • Traffic warden
- Cardiologist • Jewellery designer

LEO FRIENDS AND FAMILY

For all your outward-leaning popularity, you are a little cautious about calling someone your friend, and you're suspicious of anyone who assumes your friendship without getting to know you well. You love meeting new people and have an unusually large circle of acquaintances, but for you to declare that someone is more than an admiring hanger-on is another matter. This is partly because you feel a sense of responsibility as the leader of the group to look out for your friends — and there's only so many people you can squeeze under your wing. You also spend a great deal of time, money and energy on the people you care about, so you tend to choose wisely.

Once you decide someone is your buddy, you'll do everything in your power to be there for them. A naturally encouraging person, you'll give moral support when they need to feel brave, and a shoulder to cry on when they need your support. You're not just a trustworthy, loyal companion; you have quite the reputation for being a party animal. Nobody goes for a quiet night out with Leo. You love dancing, music, extravagant shows and cabarets, theatre, fancy restaurants and glamorous clothes. You'll encourage everyone around you to overindulge, and you'll all have a big laugh about your over-the-top antics the next day.

FAMILY PRIDE

Your home is your royal lair, your kingdom, and as a Sun-ruled person you'll like it to be filled with natural light. Potted plants, herbs and a bit of greenery will appeal, as will oversized or ostentatious furniture and some exotic touches. You are an extravagant decorator, preferring bold colours and patterns. And some original fine art will usually be on display.

An inviting den will be the heart of your home, whether you have a large family or a pet pussycat. A little vain, you may choose to display a flattering portrait of yourself, and you'll highlight any pictures of your loved ones at boastful moments — graduating, performing or meeting famous people.

You want everyone under your roof to be happy, and you see it as your responsibility to keep them all content and entertained. Home entertaining — gathering loved ones for grand dinner parties — is your forte. You love to show off your expensive taste and treat everyone to the finest fare you can afford.

LEO PARENT

A proud parent, you adore watching your children grow, explore and build confidence. You're fiercely protective of your youngsters and will see it as your job to shower them with all the love and attention you're capable of — nothing is too good for your child. You expect loyalty and obedience in return, and can feel very hurt if your offspring don't appreciate your sacrifice. But love always wins the day for Leo — a hug and some kind words work like magic, and all will be forgiven.

LEO CHILD

Fire-sign Leo children usually get what they want. When in a good mood, they are like little rays of sunlight, delightful, entertaining and eager to please, like a little cute lion cub. But when they think they're not getting enough attention, those little rays of sunlight can turn into scorching laser beams. Ignore your little Leo at your peril, as they're happy to push the boundaries and engage in power battles to find out who's really the boss. When they get older, your Leo kid may enjoy dressing outlandishly or, a born performer, putting on shows for friends and family.

HEALTHY LEO

Ruled by the life-giving Sun, you're a high-energy person with an unquenchable zest for life. You take your exercise routine seriously, partly because you're a Fire sign, and will feel more relaxed when you've burned off some of that excess zeal. But typically it's vanity that is your biggest motivator, and you know it keeps you looking so good!

Vigorous workouts and cardio routines keep your circulatory system ticking over, but you would rather be outside in the Sun and fresh air than cooped up in a gym or sports club. You can't keep a Lion indoors for long — unless they're sleeping.

Having the undivided attention of a personal trainer might be something that's hard to resist, as you'll be happy to impress someone who is there exclusively to encourage and praise you. An expert to help with your dietary requirements and a specially tailored meal plan would also gratify your need for attention, and your own personal chef would be perfect!

TEAM LEO

Fun and games are a favourite Leo pastime, whether playing cards or Monopoly at home or enjoying a sporting challenge where you can improve on your personal best, with activities like golf, tennis or interval training.

You're happiest when surrounded by other people, so being a member of a team will satisfy your social instincts. Football, basketball, hockey and most team sports will appeal and, of course, you will aim to be the star player. You expect applause and praise, but it's really your enthusiastic, spirited approach and great organizational skills that make you such a valued player.

FLAMBOYANT TASTE

If you can afford it, you'd probably choose to eat out most of the time. You get to show off your new outfit, talk to everyone and get seen in a fashionable spot. Besides, cooking and cleaning isn't really your thing. You do enjoy baking awesome-looking cakes because of the wow factor, but you'll leave all the washing up to someone else.

You prefer eating in company, and your generosity and flamboyant taste make you a perfect dinner date. When you choose something from the menu, you're usually looking for the caviar, lobster and oysters rather than anything modest — or something you have in your fridge back home. You'll go for the fanciest dish on the menu and insist on buying everyone at the table drinks.

BIG CAT DOWN TIME

Relaxing is a big deal for you, but even your down time can look pretty hectic to less energetic types. As the zodiac's favourite party animal, when you're out having fun you'll be on your feet until the music stops, you run out of alcohol or everyone leaves. But Lions need their sleep, and you can get tetchy if you haven't had a proper lie-in for a few days. You can occasionally appear lazy — but if anyone sees what you've been doing the rest of the time they'll understand why you're anything but!

Leo's preferred places
- Five-star hotels
- Beverly Hills • Palace of Versailles
- The Sphinx • Los Angeles
- Exclusive yacht party • Rio de Janeiro
- Las Vegas • Luxury spa • Theatre

VIRGO
(24 AUGUST — 23 SEPTEMBER)

Y ou were born to create order in a chaotic world, to be of service to humanity by keeping everything in good working order: sharp, clean, polished and beautifully organized. You have a defined, natural ability to know how to put things right. If you are talking to someone who has a piece of fluff on their jacket, you may not be able to concentrate on what they're saying until you have removed it. You can't help but notice inconsistencies, mistakes and small flaws in your everyday life — not out of any malice or antagonism towards others, but to improve life's functioning and make things run more smoothly for everyone.

Without you, Virgo, the world would descend into madness. You're one of the most hard-working, conscientious signs of the zodiac — and certainly the most industrious. If anyone needs to get something done, or to understand how something works, they ask you first because they know they'll receive a sensible, practical answer that's beautifully simple.

Earth signs are connected to the tangible, practical world, and in your case, as you are ruled by analytical, loquacious Mercury, your restless thinking patterns operate through your physical body. Virgo is the zodiac sign most associated with health and healing, and you are likely very aware of your own body and the need to keep it in good condition. Sometimes your mercurial concern with health can spill over into hypochondria, but more often than not it translates as a keen interest in health and nutrition and a wish to keep yourself as pure and natural as possible.

Your astrological emblem, the Virgin, relates to your shyness, idealism and desire for perfection. The Virgin is usually depicted holding sheaves of wheat in her hands, symbolizing the harvest in late summer — Virgo time. The wheat is thought to represent the wisdom she's gathered from different fields of experience.

USEFUL AND PRODUCTIVE

You work extremely hard to help other people, or to contribute to a useful cause. You're happy to work on your own without praise or recognition, as long as you're working alongside others who appreciate what you're doing. But if you feel you're tackling the world's problems alone, you'll become resentful and a little hurt. Appreciating that not everyone shares your passion for making a difference or wishes to put as much energy into making the world a better place can be a little disappointing.

You don't want to do all the work, but it would irritate you far too much to leave it to someone else who wouldn't do as good a job. But, unfortunately for you, more unscrupulous types also know you'll take care of things eventually; they may occasionally do things purposefully sloppily, knowing you will want to take that task off them next time. Your to-do lists are often full of other lists of tasks, and quite a few of those items are not really that important. But they give you a sense of purpose and help you feel that you're being productive.

KINDLY CONTROL FREAK

A kind and helpful person, you're a perfectionist at heart. You see it as your duty to help the people you love be the best they can. When you notice talent or aptitude in others, you instinctively want to encourage them to better themselves because you find wasted potential deeply upsetting. This desire for perfection and efficiency can sometimes mean you spend most of your time concentrating on things that aren't quite right or could be better.

You fuss and worry over little things and can't relax until you've reorganized and ordered what's in front of you. You're fussy about your workspace and unable to settle into writing an email if your desk is untidy or there's a coffee-mug stain on your coaster. When you cook, you wash up and clean as you go, organizing cupboards while food is in the oven. You can't lounge on the sofa until the dog's been fed, the washing machine is empty, the clothes are dry and everything's folded and put away. You probably have a very clean, tidy home but you rarely take time to appreciate it. And if you did, you'd probably notice that the walls need repainting or decide that an old picture could do with a better frame.

Deep down you may feel that if you edit down your possessions enough or do your job incredibly efficiently you will have more time in the day to do the things you love. But in reality you end up heaping more things on yourself to complete or resolve. One of the most liberating things you can do as a Virgo is to chuck your lists in the bin. Then you'll find out in time exactly what is essential and what isn't, and you won't fritter so much of your life away on trivialities.

One of your biggest fears is that if you let things go, all will descend into madness. You can't put your partner in charge of dinner or take up your housemate's offer to take care of the laundry because the results will not please you. But if you want your life back, and are drowning in chores, you must learn to delegate — and you may even have to try to live with some compromises.

BE KINDER TO YOURSELF

You're a champion at singing other people's praises and helping them grow and express their talents, but you keep your own mighty capabilities to yourself. Modest to your core, you can be extremely hard on yourself. The idea that you might be held up to others' criticism makes you feel very uneasy.

Above all, you are compelled to be honest, and showing off in any way would be tantamount to declaring yourself perfect — something your own high standards just won't allow you to do. Even if your brilliance is obvious to everyone around you, you'll still have cause to doubt it.

VIRGO IN LOVE

You are a naturally private person, so when you first realize you are attracted to another, it can take you a little by surprise. You are picky, but that's just because you know what you're looking for — so when you see someone who fits the bill, it's a bit unsettling. You might not even understand what you're supposed to do next.

You're naturally shy in love, and you often have a crush for a long time before you pluck up the courage to act on it, if at all!

Prone to self-criticism, you'll probably have come up with a hundred reasons why your beloved won't be interested. You hold yourself to the same high standards you expect from a lover, and it can be difficult for you to live up to your own self-imposed rules. But if you could stand back and take an honest look at yourself or have a bit of faith in what others are telling you, then you may notice the charming, self-effacing, kind and talented person who everyone sees.

THOUGHTFUL AND ATTENTIVE

Once in a relationship, you are committed. As an Earth sign, you need security and loyalty from your partner and wish for a comfortable life where you can grow and learn from each other. Your planetary ruler, Mercury, looks for friendship, and an intellectual rapport is crucial to the longevity of your partnership. You're a thoughtful, attentive lover and, surprisingly, considering your virginal symbolism, when you're under the sheets you're a passionate and adventurous lover.

You want your life together to be private, and you expect the same level of discretion from your partner. You won't be happy if you find out your other half has been posting pictures of your life together on social media; you'll even feel uncomfortable discussing details of your love life with your friends and family.

You value honesty over flattery and would much rather hear constructive criticism instead of meaningless compliments. Knowing what your other half really thinks is far more important to you than being told what you want to hear, and it will bring you closer together.

For a truly blissful relationship, your partner ought to understand how your mind works. If he or she knows you well, they'll appreciate that for you to feel relaxed and focused on them, your environment should be neat and orderly. Your lover becomes much sexier in your eyes if they voluntarily take out the bins or dry the cutlery before putting it away. A self-respecting true Virgo will feel a thrill of satisfaction seeing their other half scrubbing grouting with bleach and a toothbrush.

Most compatible love signs

PISCES Pisces hypnotize you with their unending faith in love, and will help you let go and trust in life's essential goodness.

VIRGO As long as you are not too intellectually competitive, this ought to be a very stimulating and nurturing relationship.

TAURUS You have a similar work ethic and values, and agree that love is a life-long commitment.

DISTRACTING PERFECTION

You notice all the little details about your partner, from where they buy their shoes to how they like their eggs and which toothpaste they prefer. You show a touching concern that their lives are running smoothly, and readily offer assistance. You take your routines and rituals seriously and expect your loved ones to feel the same way. If the person you adore always has crumpets for breakfast and you've only got porridge, you'll make an early-morning trip to find crumpets. You'll have catalogued all your lover's favourite things, and even when they're not sure which brand of socks they prefer or what they need on holiday, you will have the answer.

You can get so absorbed in making life perfect for your partner that you can lose sight of what you

Least compatible love signs

ARIES Impulsive Fire signs prefer to do things rather than talk about them — so no long nights spent discussing your ingrown toenails with them, then.

SAGITTARIUS Sweeping generalizations drive you potty.

LIBRA You respect people with honest opinions that they stand by, and Libra changes theirs depending on who they last spoke to.

need from the relationship. Mercury-ruled people love to learn new things and to better themselves, so discovering a different language together, hiking or taking an interest in nutrition are productive pastimes that will make you feel like you are healthy and growing as a couple.

TRICKY EMOTIONS

You pursue perfection gently, perhaps even a little unconsciously. But it's important that you recognize this trait and make peace with it, because if you don't, it could drive you quite mad. Noticing small things that unsettle you can build imperceptibly until one day your partner accidentally sneezes over your dinner or leaves the nail clippers in the bed and *bang!* — you're divorced! Deep down, one of your biggest fears is that you're imperfect, and maybe that's why you're so harsh on yourself and exacting of the people around you. One of your greatest lessons is to accept your own failings, for when you do, you'll relax and be much more tolerant of everyone else's. Everyone is flawed and still lovable — even you!

VIRGO AT WORK

You're a hard-working problem-solver, famed for your clear, uncluttered communication style. Meticulous by nature, you like to assimilate the task in front of you, piece by piece, and analyze the information in minute detail. Your thoroughness is unique in the workplace, and when given a job to do, you treat it seriously. It might take a while longer to complete than the other zodiac signs, because you will correct and adjust every error as you go, but the end result will be impeccable. This applies whether you're an accountant, a florist or a trombone player.

RIGHT, OR LIKED?

If you're honest, Virgo, you probably realize you make more work for yourself than you need to. You are always busy, but you tend to be the only one adding things to your in-tray. It's your raison d'être to consider and evaluate, and your reverence for productivity can mean you labour over technicalities. Every stage of your work matters, and you have a logical, thought-out opinion about what you're doing and why. But your conscientiousness can take up more time than you like, which just makes you more anxious that details might get missed if you rush it.

You're not an aggressive person by any means, but if you think you're right (and you usually are), you won't back down. That's not because you are being antagonistic, it is because you are right!

This can frustrate less fastidious co-workers. Doggedly pointing out that your boss has made a mistake may well give you the moral high ground, but it won't always make you very popular. Whether you want to be right or you want to be liked is a dilemma you will probably face at some point in your career.

POWER BEHIND THE THRONE

You are often happier working behind the scenes, even when you and everyone around you knows you're actually the one in charge. For all your conviction in your opinions, you can be surprisingly shy about assuming a position of authority. This is because you're such a scrupulously honest person that pretending to be something or someone you're not is almost impossible. Brasher, more egotistical Sun signs will assume authority without a shred of your knowledge or expertise (or modesty), but when the spotlight shines on you, you feel your confidence ebb away.

Perhaps you feel more useful helping other people perfect and hone their skills rather than being the star player. After all, Virgo is, in a rather old-fashioned way, referred to as the sign of 'service'. You're OK being the power behind the throne, where you're the one doing all the clever stuff, but someone else is shouting about it. You might be demure and self-effacing, but you accept and expect credit for a job well done.

When you are the one in charge, you're usually an exacting but considerate boss. You love to see people better themselves and take your advice. An excellent teacher when you know someone is willing to learn, you are patient, kind and supportive. You don't mean your criticisms to be taken personally because when someone appraises your own work, you genuinely use it as an opportunity to improve. Not everyone feels the same, though, and maybe emphasizing what the people in your charge are doing right will encourage them far more than pointing out their weak spots.

WHERE YOU EXCEL

Virgo is associated with health and healing, ensuring all the complex parts of the body are functioning properly together. Therefore, combining your Mercury-ruled capacity for knowledge with your earthy, natural ability to work with something tangible in a career as a doctor, surgeon or nutritionist would suit you well.

Your dedication and meticulous skills see you excel in tasks that require detailed or exacting standards. Science, maths, engineering and editing work would all satisfy your analytical brain and eagle-eyed abilities.

Your discernment, discretion and grasp of minutiae would be an asset if you took up law, or even if you were appointed as a judge. After all, nobody loves the last word more than a Virgo!

Perfect Virgo careers
- Computer engineer
- Laboratory assistant
- Nutritionist • Life coach
- Accountant • Restaurant critic
- Proofreader • Air-traffic controller
- Journalist • Veterinarian

VIRGO FRIENDS AND FAMILY

A little reticent in social situations, you can take some time to feel comfortable with new people. But when you do relax, you're witty, warm and talkative. A devoted Earth sign, when you decide someone is your friend you are loyal to that person through the good times and the bad. You give the best advice, from how to remove tomato-soup stains from wool carpets to buying a new home. You have the latest information at your fingertips, and you love a lively discussion about it with your buddies. Your sensible, nuanced opinions mean you're a trusted confidante. Your friends know how deeply you care about them — even if you are sometimes so exacting or finicky that it drives them to distraction!

Certainly the most thoughtful gift buyer in the zodiac, you have an astonishing memory for the little things that make people happy. You probably have lists of the items your friends have expressed a preference for at some point and will always make a mental note of their favourite colours, foods, designers and artists.

Introverted, but driven by the urge to communicate and connect, you're not usually the first person on the dancefloor at parties, but you do manage to talk to everyone in the room. Needing to feel useful, you avoid awkward socializing by being the person helping out — passing around the nibbles or volunteering to tackle the washing up at the end of the night.

MINIMALIST MINDSET

When in your own home, you let your hair down, although what you mean by relaxing can look a little control-freaky to the other zodiac signs. Clutter and disorder make you uneasy, and your home — whether it's a room in a shared apartment or a large house with a garden — is usually spotless, neat and simple, or quite possibly spartan and bare!

Preferring minimal arrangements, you're not one for expensive, fussy or elaborate decoration. You know without having to think about it where everything in your home is, because every item has a use and a place — and if it doesn't, you'll donate it to charity or give it to a friend. You only keep what you need; otherwise you spend too much of your time organizing your stuff, which you find both addictive and anxiety-inducing. At some point in your life you may have had a passion for cleaning or ordering that's borderline obsessive. Saying that, you are surprisingly comfortable in other people's messier spaces, and are actually rather brilliant at helping them tackle their haphazard hoards. But your own home or workspace has to be shipshape and functioning to reflect your inner hankering for order.

PASSION FOR PETS

Pets are an important part of Virgo life. Perhaps it's your affinity with healing the body that, for some reason lost to astrological obscurity, your sign is associated with 'small animals'. Looking after a cat, dog or rabbit brings you a great deal of pleasure and companionship, and you will happily accommodate them in your daily routine. Without you, Virgo, your partner, family, housemates or pets would be living in a chaotic hellhole with a sink full of cat food.

VIRGO PARENT

As the sign of service, parenting comes easily to you, and you selflessly tend to put the needs of others before your own. You're a loving and attentive parent, keenly interested in your child's development and education. Wishing to bring out the very best in your offspring, you may have to bite your tongue when your inner critic takes hold.

VIRGO CHILD

Virgo youngsters can be a little cautious or shy, preferring to observe what is going on before they get involved. They're usually highly intelligent, curious and sharp, and, when they get interested in something, are very talkative indeed! Virgo kids can be fidgety and picky about their food, but they adore reading and it usually has a calming effect.

HEALTHY VIRGO

Virgo is the zodiac sign most connected with health, habits and routine, so looking after your wellbeing will be high on your agenda. You don't get bored as easily as the other zodiac signs, so repetitive exercise keeps you happily ticking over. You appreciate that those little movements all add up, and you'll be tenaciously determined to smash through your personal bests. Activities that test your endurance and suit your quick, nimble gait, such as hiking, distance running and swimming, will help you feel energized and burn off some of that mental restlessness you're so prone to.

You're a stickler for progress. Spreadsheets, nutrition specs and stats, wearable devices and fitness productivity tools should make things more interesting. And keeping an online log of your routines and targets will help you chart your progress. You're the fitness bunny at the gym who has all the gear and knows how to use it.

CAREFUL CONSUMER

As the zodiac sign that's most connected with digestion, you have a sensitive constitution, and you feel out of sorts when you're not eating correctly. Often the most clued-up person on nutrition and healthy eating, you are not impressed by junk food. You are more likely to be vegan or vegetarian than most, and you insist on the best-quality ingredients you can afford — preferably local, organic and in season. You enjoy cooking but are suspicious of fatty, sugary or processed products. It's usually easier for you to eat at home as you can be a fussy eater in restaurants, but you do enjoy talking with friends while you cook.

You like to keep yourself relatively pure, so you won't last the distance on a boozy night out. But a glass or two of Champagne or excellent wine will hit the spot from time to time. That's when your nearest and dearest see the more relaxed version of you, and you can be hilariously witty when you're not feeling self-conscious. Generally, though, you're a juicing, raw-food and steamed-vegetable aficionado whose idea of a Friday-night treat is a bag of assorted nuts!

PRACTICE ESCAPISM

Stress and anxiety are often your greatest health challenges. It's so hard for you to switch off that constant instinct to learn, improve and be productive that you often work late or take work home with you. But being a slave to perfection can take its toll. You can become anxious about underperforming, even if you're actually doing more than everyone else. Then, when you get tired, you can't see the wood for the trees, and you can get hung up on one small thing that keeps you awake at night.

You must learn to unwind. Switch off your phone, hide away your laptop and lists and try some meditation, yoga or, even better, a bit of mental escapism such as a good book or a movie. You spend so much of your time looking after everyone else that you can't see when you're the one in need of a cuddle, a candlelit bath and an early night.

Virgo's preferred places
- Silent retreat • Pilates bootcamp
- Cycling holiday • Exotic cookery course
- Extreme exercise bootcamp
- Holistic massage break
- Horse-riding school
- Personal-development course
- Wine-tasting trip • Book fair

LIBRA
(24 SEPTEMBER — 23 OCTOBER)

You are an intellectual Air sign ruled by romantic, charming Venus. As an Air sign, you are one of the zodiac's thinkers and communicators, and with relationship-oriented Venus as your ruler, you crave harmonious rapport, balance and fairness with everyone you encounter. You are one of the most sociable signs of the zodiac, and your desire to please others and dislike of conflict mean you sometimes sacrifice your own ambitions to keep the peace. Your astrological symbol is the Scales, representing your fair judgment, excellent taste and love of symmetry. Because you are concerned with making the right decision, it can take you a long time to weigh up all the options, but when you have made up your mind, it's usually set in stone... unless too many people disagree with you, in which case you may have to rethink!

THE QUEST FOR LOVE AND RELATIONSHIPS

As the seventh of the 12 zodiac signs, you are the first to have an opposite number, and your longing for a partner is one of your strongest motivations. You were born to share, discuss and consider your thoughts and feelings with others, and you need strong relationships to make you feel more complete. It's natural for you to

ponder others' opinions before you make up your own
mind — even if you don't necessarily agree with them.
Bouncing ideas back against someone else somehow
makes your own thoughts feel more solid and real. You
find it easier to see yourself through the eyes of other
people, so their good opinion seems essential if you are
to have good opinion of yourself.

Ruled by affectionate, amorous Venus, romantic
love is one of your highest priorities. You are usually
either in love or pursuing a new romance. And your
relationship with your other half will usually dominate
your thoughts. As a mentally focused Air sign, you are
in love with the idea of love — yearning for another,
the uniting of soulmates, and the wonder of romantic
possibilities. Sex is, of course, a beautiful part of the
deal, but the physical aspects of love aren't usually as
important to you than the companionship, friendliness
and sharing.

If you have a preponderance of independent Fire
signs in your birth char,t you may not be as dependent
on others for your happiness, as a true Libra often is.
It's important that you spend some of your time living
alone, so that you learn you can be truly happy without
a significant other. It's all too easy for you to feel bonded
to others' opinions, likes and fears, but the answers
to what you want from life can only come from deep
within you.

To help you discover who you really are, you may,
quite unconsciously, see others as a mirror. This can

sometimes mean you remain with a partner for too long, out of the fear of being alone. However, when you let yourself explore different types of relationships with a variety of people, you will discover how you differ from them, and what makes you unique. It's often a balancing act between you and others, and your thoughts and emotions. But weighing things up is what you were born to do!

BEAUTY IN ALL THINGS

Both Taurus and Libra are Venus-ruled and have a deep appreciation for beauty and the finer things in life. Taurus is an Earth sign, so their love tends to be expressed through a desire for tangible things, such as food, comfort and money. In Air sign Libra, your Venusian sensibilities are conveyed though the expression of ideas — intellectual compatibility, wit, excellent manners, refined tastes, intelligence and appearance. You can be quite particular about how you decorate and beautify your environment — and yourself!

You may refuse to answer the door if you think you're looking shabby. Even in a hospital bed, you'll be the cute one with shiny hair, stylish pyjamas, designer stubble or full make-up. You dress well and are a dedicated follower of fashion, enjoying colour, eye-catching designs and sumptuous fabrics. Style usually trumps comfort in your eyes, and you'll plump for gorgeous shoes over uglier, more practical varieties every time. Your luxury-loving Venusian tastes often stretch your budget, but you'll gladly go into the red for a beautiful bit of tailoring. You have an outfit for every occasion and you always notice what other people are wearing.

Your environment needs to reflect your refined tastes too, and your home will be a clutter-free, peaceful space, artfully decorated and aesthetically pleasing. Fresh flowers, candles and some contemporary works of art will adorn your perfectly painted walls.

CHAMPAGNE TASTE ON A PAUPER'S BUDGET?

Venus is the planet most associated with money, but whereas the other Venus sign, Taurus, tends to save carefully and sensibly, you're in awe of all the luxurious and enjoyable items that money allows you to experience — that's what you think credit cards are for! You rival extravagant Leo as one the zodiac's most lavish spenders, and if you have enough in the black, you see it as money to be spent rather than saved or invested.

You live for your social life and, when you have it, you lend and spend on your friends so that everyone can enjoy the good times with you. Amazing holidays, gorgeous clothes and fine dining all feature prominently in your spending habits. You see money as the way to make your life more exciting and glamorous now, rather than waiting to be able to afford enjoyable new things. You love quality and style but you're not a rash spender, frittering away small amounts or living in denial of your bank balance. You're perfectly clear about where it all goes — and you enjoy every penny!

TO BE FAIR

As you are the sign of balance, and the zodiac's diplomat, you insist you hear all sides of a story before deciding what the fairest course of action should be. An excellent listener, you empathize with everyone's account and don't take immediate action before you have considered all options. You try to be as impartial as possible, which wins you many friends, and you always know all the gossip because the people around you genuinely value your judgment and share all the juicy details.

Your instinctive peace-making skills do sometimes come at a price, though, as constantly seeing things from other people's points of view can obscure your own feelings and be at the expense of your own swift and dynamic decision-making. People-pleasing is such second nature to you that you lose sight of your own power to decide where to go, and with whom. Your exceptional tolerance can sometimes lead others to take advantage of your good nature — or they might assume you will always back them up. Often fearing to rock the boat too much, less scrupulous individuals can become frustrated with your passivity, and can goad you into making decisions that you're not quite ready for.

Always giving people the benefit of the doubt is an admirable personality trait, as long as you are dealing with people who have equally high morals. At some point in your life you may find yourself in a far-from-perfect relationship, or a situation where you have continued, uncomplaining and forgiving, for months or years. On an unconscious level you may have been registering that things are not working, but the scales haven't quite tipped one way or the other. Then, quite out of the blue, after a small disagreement, you suddenly tip — your mind is made up and there's no going back.

LIBRA IN LOVE

You're an old-fashioned romantic, Libra, and you want the whole fairy tale! You're an intellectual Air sign ruled by Venus, the love and relationship planet, so searching for romantic fulfilment is a crucial part of your existence. Libra is the sign of partnership, of looking at the world from outside of oneself, and a true Libra will long to meet their soulmate.

You love the drama and ceremony of romance, and you absolutely expect to find it. But because this is such an important aspect of your life, you may take an inordinately long time to make up your mind about exactly what you're looking for in a life partner. It's just too important a decision to be made lightly.

FLIRTY AND CHARMING

Your attractive, sociable personality and comely smile ensure you won't be short of admirers. If someone takes your fancy, you'll weigh up the pros and cons before finding out more about him or her. You take great pleasure in the more genteel aspects of courtship, but you can be extremely seductive when you're attracted to someone — and very hard to resist!

Your intended will be able to keep you entertained with their wit, and as a loquacious Air sign you get a kick out of sending flirty messages back and forth. A potential partner has to appeal to you mentally, perhaps even as something of a fantasy figure, before you'll up your game.

Going on romantic dates, sending each other thoughtful gifts and letting yourself be chased and wooed are all thrilling stages of true love for you. The excitement of the initial swoony passion of a new love affair, where you both crash into lamp-posts daydreaming of the other, is your rose-tinted Libra idea of heaven. Once you've weighed up all the possibilities and decided to go for it, you shower your other half with love and attention. You're thoughtful and affectionate and always thinking up ways to please the one you adore.

EQUALITY AND SHARING

Disliking chaos, discord and negativity, you are very sensitive to any of your partner's criticism and you worry about what they really think. It's important for you both to be able to talk candidly at the start of a relationship and to pledge always to communicate. You need reassurance that everything is going well, and you can become resentful if you're on the end of any silent treatment without knowing precisely why. You must feel that you're an equal partner and are not solely responsible for your beloved's good — or bad — moods.

Most compatible love signs

GEMINI The good-natured banter you share will keep you both in stitches, and you'll always be able to surprise each other.

AQUARIUS Social Aquarius enjoys your wit and charm and learns from your people-pleasing skills, while Aquarius teaches you how to be less concerned about what others think.

LEO You're a two-person party! You both love the limelight and being seen at your best, but you can laze about in style together too.

Least compatible love signs

CANCER You have some trouble understanding each other's emotions, as your feelings propel you towards people while Cancer's make them scuttle away.

CAPRICORN Solemn Capricorns make you laugh with their dry sense of humour, but they're naturally reserved and haughty, whereas you're effusive and open.

VIRGO You get on well as friends, as you both appreciate excellent craftsmanship and notice details others miss. But Virgo's a realist and you're a romantic.

Togetherness is your favourite thing, and snuggling up on the sofa with your other half for a lazy night in is one of your favourite things, as long as there's good-quality nibbles, wine and an arty film in the offing. But you also love showing your lover off. You're a sociable type who enjoys dressing up to be seen in the hottest places, and you'll want to share the glam high life with your chosen companion.

TRICKY EMOTIONS

You feel deeply unsettled by angry scenes, chaos and noise, so you shy away from conflict or arguments. If your partner says something harsh, or if they're loud and angry, you find it difficult to respond. Arguments and ugly scenes have you running for the hills. Your politeness prevents you from being outspoken even when you feel you ought to be sticking up for yourself. It feels so uncomfortable when your sense of harmony is disrupted that you'll make peace as quickly as possible — even if you're not in the wrong.

Your fear of confrontation can occasionally be used against you by less scrupulous types, and not being able to voice your anger can make you feel powerless. Being completely honest with your lover is a challenge, not only because of the unbearable tension, but because of your indecisiveness and unwillingness to take any action.

Telling others exactly where you stand is probably a skill you'll learn from experience. But life will get easier once you realize that the sky doesn't fall down if you voice an opinion, and others will respect you for being honest.

LIBRA AT WORK

Behind your sweet, sociable personality lies a shrewd business brain. As one of the zodiac's most skilled communicators, you understand how to persuade people to work together, and you're one of the few signs of the zodiac who really knows how to delegate. Well-liked in the workplace, you go out of your way to please your co-workers and easily make friends at the office. Colleagues know you to be a friendly, chilled and witty character, and you're actually surprisingly cool and logical when faced with stressful or complicated tasks. Sharp, clever and creative, you are as good at knitting the details together as you are at spotting errors.

Seeking balance in all things, you're neither a workaholic nor lazy, and you seek to level your industriousness with after-work drinks, laughter and cake. Your office or desk is usually the most fun place for your co-workers to hang out, and your love of sharing extends to salacious gossip. You're happy to assist co-workers who need a helping hand and will listen patiently to their woes with a sympathetic ear. You form life-long friends in the workplace — from the post boy to the CEO, and you treat everyone with the same easy respect and cordial good humour.

MAKING THE WORLD MORE BEAUTIFUL

Your Venusian ruler compels you to create a more harmonious and beautiful world. Artistic and creative, you have an affinity with good design that's user-friendly, and you might enjoy building sleek websites or working as a graphic designer. Your eye for colour and desire for pleasant surroundings might spur you on to become an interior designer or architect, and many Libras work in the music and fashion industries. The beauty industry may appeal too, especially if combined with more social aspects of the job. Life as a make-up artist, costume designer, hairdresser or masseuse should be enjoyable, as you could combine your social and artistic abilities. Your celebrated interpersonal skills open up public relations as an option, and resolving conflicts and being a trusted mediator would see you excel in a human resources department.

Driven by an obsession with fairness, becoming a lawyer would channel your Libran wish for justice. Your natural charisma and charm would be helpful in gaining clients' trust, and your Air-sign talent for communication would help you make an impact in the courtroom.

BALANCING AT THE TOP

You're a very friendly, sociable boss, not altogether comfortable being the one making all the difficult decisions. You can labour over the smallest choices, but when you make your judgment, your opinion is usually nuanced and well-respected. You make it very easy for your co-workers to communicate with you, and honest communication is heartily encouraged. Though it can sometimes be hard for you to draw the line between what's popular and what actually works, your style is very open because you wish for everyone to see that you are doing your utmost to make things work. This approach can sometimes be time-consuming, as you have to wait for democratic agreement and compromise, but you wouldn't be convinced of the ethics of anything too dictatorial.

Your clever charm means you can turn someone down for a pay rise but have them leave your office feeling better about themselves than when they went in. Less charitable colleagues may say your friendliness can get in the way of your work, but the opposite is usually true. When you need something done, people around you are happy to help, as they'll be keen to repay past favours.

Perfect Libra careers
• Human resources
• Relationship counsellor　• Web designer
• Make-up artist　• Hairdresser
• Public-relations consultant
• Art dealer　• Event planner
• Lawyer　• Fashion designer

LIBRA FRIENDS AND FAMILY

You're a dedicated people person, and making friends is one of your most appealing talents. It's an area where your confidence shines, and you remember little details about new people that make them feel included and special. Your interest in others is sincere, and is the reason you'll have such a large pool of loyal pals from all walks of life. With a natural ability to ask the right questions, make them laugh and bring them out of their shell, even your most introverted friends bend to your charming insistence that they spend time with you.

Clued up on what's trendy, fun or interesting, you know the best places to be seen and will thoroughly enjoy a night on the town. The ritual of getting ready for a glamorous occasion with your buddies is something of a Libra speciality. Both sexes turn the preamble to going out into an art form, with music, cocktails and a thousand wardrobe changes. For a more low-key affair, you're happy to make your pals feel comfortable in your home. You're a generous and thoughtful host, and will set up sophisticated cocktails, exceptional appetisers and flattering lighting for a relaxing but elegant heart-to-heart.

FAMILY DYNAMICS

You view your home as an extension of your artistic talents, whether it's a bedsit or a swanky country house. Your taste is exquisite, and you'll have plenty of beautiful objects on display. Even more modest Libra homes will have a couple of designer pieces, elegant furniture or gorgeously sumptuous fabrics on show. Comfort is important, but looking the part is essential! Your taste changes often, and you regularly appraise whether your decor is reflecting your current tastes. Your restlessness and artistic standards can get a little frustrating for others, but living with you is usually so pleasant that your partner, housemates or family all tolerate your constantly evolving ideas of what looks right or good.

As the sign of relationships, you'll likely be keen to start a family. But because you're so enamoured with romance, you'll be keen to keep your love story glowing throughout parenthood.

Your home must be tranquil, as you expect everyone in it to be as sensitive to bad atmospheres as you are. You like to remind the people who share your space how special they are and will have plenty of photographs of loved ones dotted around. Always balancing extremes, if your home or family life becomes too complacent, you'll announce a surprising trip or treat for everyone. And if things become too chaotic, you'll be the peacemaker calming everyone down.

LIBRA PARENT

Disliking authoritarian rules, you can be a laid-back parent who wants to be friends with your kids first and foremost. You tend to leave difficult conversations to the other adults, and concentrate on being a loveable, fun pal. This can sometimes mean you create blurred boundaries, which can be confusing for you all. Best to stick to a 'firm but fair' policy, where you all know what's expected from each other.

LIBRA CHILD

Emotionally intelligent and sensitive to negativity, little Libra senses when their parents are upset, which can cause them to get clingy. It's tricky for mini-Libra to understand that saying 'no' to them doesn't mean they're not loved. Helping your Libra kids understand that their intense or difficult emotions are healthy will be both challenging and very rewarding.

HEALTHY LIBRA

You love to look hot, Libra, and it can be a challenge for you to balance your love of food and full social life with a limiting diet or rigorous exercise plan. Venus-ruled signs are usually well groomed and spend a great deal of care on their appearance, so getting hot, sweaty and breathless won't be your first choice when it comes to staying active. Ugliness disturbs you, and you can be harsh on yourself if you catch an unflattering glimpse of your puffy, straining face in a mirror. If you wish to feel balanced and happy, you will want to feel that you're not depriving yourself — after all, is life really worth living if there are no champagne cocktails or chocolate truffles?

FOOD AND DRINK

Venus is a planet of enjoyment, and food will be high on your agenda. Venus-ruled Taurus and Libra both have quite slow metabolisms and are prone to gaining weight. Sweets, puddings and carbs are one of your greatest pleasures, but obviously there is a downside to all those delicious treats. Your busy social schedule means you're often at the mercy of other people's cooking, or exquisite menus in delightfully indulgent restaurants. It's hard to be disciplined when there's such an abundance of delicious goodies on show. Cakes, sweets and calorific bakery goods tend to be your favourite way to reward yourself, so you're unlikely to plump for a green salad when you're congratulating yourself on reaching a personal goal.

Balance is the key to your wellbeing, and your passion for indulgent food may be difficult to master, but there is a middle road. Air signs dislike feeling heavy after rich food, as it saps your vitality and makes you feel lazy. You can address the sluggishness by eating smaller portions and keeping your food choices interesting. Or perhaps when you are at home you can decide to prepare healthier but tasty options for yourself, but choose whatever you fancy from the menu when you're out for dinner.

ACTIVITIES AND RELAXATION

The gym doesn't hold much appeal — unless it's a cool place to hang out, in which case you'll enjoy spending time in the cafe, chatting to friends and blowing your hard-earned calories over lunch. If you do venture onto some machines, you'll be wearing the latest kit and will sneak a good look at what other people are wearing too. As the sign of relationships, you prefer to work out with other people, so having a personal trainer or working out alone isn't for you. Tennis and squash, or any sports or activities requiring a partner, will suit your need to work with someone else, so ballroom dancing, Zumba and water-aerobics classes appeal too.

To relax and unwind, talking with friends is your preferred way to chill. Talking out any problems and knowing that someone else understands where you're coming from is the best therapy. Counselling can also work brilliantly for you if you wish to express what's on your mind directly, without worrying about offending anyone or being too polite about how you really feel.

Libra's preferred places
- Swanky nightclub • Aurora-spotting trip
- Paris • Beverly Hills
- Seychelles • French patisserie
- Miami • Gstaad • St Barts • Ibiza

SCORPIO
(24 OCTOBER — 22 NOVEMBER)

Your reputation precedes you, Scorpio. Hypnotic, sexy and mysterious with that violent sting in your tail, you appear to have all the zodiac's the most extreme and exciting personality traits. But where do these dark and dubious characteristics come from, and do you deserve them?

Scorpio is a Water sign, which is associated with strong emotions. Your planetary ruler is deep, dark, powerful Pluto, the lord of the underworld, controlling all that lies below the surface. The positive side of Pluto is that he pulls things from the dark into the light, so they can be transformed and healed. The darker side of Pluto reveals an obsession with power and control, which brings up deep passions: possessiveness, jealousy and revenge. Like your zodiac symbol, the Scorpion, you prefer to hide yourself and keep your motives secret, but you will strike if you are threatened.

STILL WATERS RUN DEEP

Enmeshed in dark myths and dramatic life-or-death symbolism, it's forgiveable to imagine Scorpio to be heartless and cruel. But your tough exterior is just armour that protects your deeply sensitive Water-sign heart. You feel your emotions very deeply, but you won't let just anyone see you vulnerable. You have a knack for unearthing other people's emotional weak spots and remembering just where to hurt them if they betray you in future. So no, you won't display your softer side, at least not without a reciprocal exchange of vulnerabilities. It's a little like owning a nuclear deterrent. When you really trust someone, they'll know where you hurt, and you'll know where they hurt. If one of you pushes the other's button, you'll destroy each other. But it takes you a long time to get to that stage of trust.

SECRETS AND TRUST

You project an almost deadpan expression, appearing extremely well-controlled, intelligent and cool as a cucumber. But a particularly observant person will notice little signs that you're covering something up. White knuckles perhaps, tension in the jaw, or maybe a slight tremor in the voice if you're really upset. But there won't usually be much to allude to the boiling mass of lava-hot feelings you're just about managing to control.

You're a secretive person, and it serves you well. When you gain someone's trust you take it as an honour. If a friend wishes to share that they're actually a spy or enjoy dressing up as a chicken for kicks, you'll take this knowledge to the grave. You keep secrets because knowledge is power, and — who knows? — you may need to use it against them one day. But it's much more likely you'll keep quiet because trust is everything to you. That's why you rely on so few people. You'll enjoy hearing salacious gossip as much as anyone, but you treat real secrets with the utmost respect.... and you will have a few of your own.

THE POWER OF MONEY

Scorpio is one of the financial zodiac signs, the other being your opposite number, Taurus. As a Pluto person, you respect the power of money and your relationship to it can be complicated. You're smart and shrewd, and you tend to make money easily, and Scorpio is also associated with inheritance, so you may benefit from a legacy of some sort. You're quite secretive about how much money you make; you won't be the one in the office discussing your annual bonus or how much your salary went up or down. But you'll be very interested in what other people are earning.

You have refined tastes and an eye for luxury goods — you'll know expensive artwork, cars or antiques when you see them, and may even splash out on some investment pieces yourself. You're not usually a careless spender, and you'll feel quite anxious if you're digging into a credit card. You understand exactly what money can buy, and safety and financial security are two of your top priorities. You often have an amount in the bank that you don't allow yourself to fall below — and you're self-controlled enough to stick to your guns.

You may plead poverty on a night out, saying you're down to your last penny, but you'll probably have paid for your home outright and have a cosy bank balance

and an impressive pension. But that's your business —
nobody else's.

In a personal birth chart, the eighth house is ruled
by Scorpio, the area connected with 'death, sex and
other people's money'... again — always with the drama!
You are considered more likely than most to benefit
from joint financial ventures, or you may excel in
careers where you look after other people's resources.

OBSESSIVE AND SEXY

When you get interested in a subject, idea or person,
you become quite obsessive. You're the person who
binge-watches episodes of a dark, gripping TV series,
stays up all night reading an absorbing detective story
or has a sudden fascination with hypnosis or mysticism.
Unlike most, you don't seem to get bored — only more
interested. This addictive quality can also seep into your
love life, where you may become obsessed by someone
you know or, occasionally, a complete stranger.

But your fascination with sex isn't purely physical.
You long to merge with someone else, to be possessed
and lose your sense of individuality in a uniting of souls,
to be born again. You don't just want sex; you're on
a quest to attain a higher level of consciousness. No
pressure on your partner, then!

SCORPIO IN LOVE

In love, you're all or nothing. Pluto-ruled people
aren't wishy-washy or coy, but you have undeniable

sex appeal. You're sultry and moody, and when you're attracted to someone new, you hint at the passionate depths you're usually so keen to conceal.

Most compatible love signs

CANCER Sensitive, intuitive Cancer can provide you with the security and reassurance you seek, and read your changing moods.

TAURUS Taurus's languid, slow, sensuous approach to life masks inner passions that attract and intrigue you.

CAPRICORN Responsible, steady goat people won't spring any surprises on you emotionally, and they're usually quite sensible with money.

Least compatible love signs

LIBRA You're too hot to handle for superficial Libra, who likes things to be nice rather than terrifyingly passionate and sweaty.

LEO The king of brash meets the king of subtle — you're made of different stuff, and won't see eye to eye for long.

ARIES You like Aries self-belief and boldness, but they lack your emotional finesse, which you can find quite annoying.

Your clothes tend to be plain, in darker colours, but you choose sensual fabrics with a touch of drama, a subtle shine, velvet trim or an upturned collar. But it's your alluring, magnetic eyes that really draw people in. Sometimes your intensity can make people feel a little uncomfortable, but it's not intentional. You look directly into people's eyes for a fraction too long, often quite unconsciously, because that's where you discover their most precious secrets. Some people feel exposed in your gaze, while others enjoy feeling seen.

STILL WATERS RUN DEEP

Seductive but subtle, when you're attracted to someone your feelings will be strong, but you probably won't want to show your hand for a while. You like to watch from afar, noticing all the intimate details of the person who has captured your attention. You take in the way they move, how they use their hands when they speak and the timbre of his or her voice. You may be having a conversation, but you've lost the thread because you've been staring at their knees, neck or lips and wondering what it would be like to kiss them. You may try to keep your feelings to yourself, but your eyes will give you away. You have a hypnotic intensity when you're looking at someone you want, and that longing stare may reveal your real feelings.

You'll be looking for signs of reciprocation, but because you're so subtle, the other person may have picked up a vibe but won't be entirely sure — unless you have Fire-sign planets in your birth chart, who declare their feelings honestly and boldly, or loquacious Air-sign placements helping you find the words to get their message across. Otherwise, you'll wait and watch — and hope they feel it too.

SEX: TRUST OR BUST

You take love seriously and don't make it easy for others to get close to you. The trust and security must be real before you let down your defences. As the zodiac's most passionate sign, you give yourself to your partner completely. For you, sex isn't purely physical; it's an all-consuming, profound spiritual union and a release of powerful reserves of emotional energy. This is not something you take lightly, as your lover will see you at your most vulnerable, so you will need plenty of reassurance that this will last forever.

Contrary to your reputation as a philanderer, you have a deep need for security and permanence in your relationships. Sex is essential to you, but you're no flash in the pan. If the love is real, you commit every fibre of your being to your partner loyally and, at times, almost obsessively. You can become possessive of your partner if they make you feel insecure, and can become very jealous if provoked. But emotionally, you give everything, so if your partner cheats, shames you or breaks your heart, you will want revenge. And the best revenge of all is to find a way not to care.

TRICKY EMOTIONS

You work harder than any other zodiac sign to repair yourself if you've been emotionally wounded. Because you are so brave and honest with yourself, you have the power to regenerate, heal and to put yourself back stronger than before. But in order to be reborn, first you have to die. You do this by fully experiencing your pain, reliving it, feeling the emotions as fully as possible, giving yourself over to the truth of the loss, rejection, fear or anger. You go deep into the well of feeling, then analyze yourself over and over for a way through. You don't always find easy answers, and sometimes there are none, but eventually, sometimes after many years, you come out healed and transformed.

SCORPIO AT WORK

Strong-willed and magnetic, you're a motivated self-starter with an aura of mystery. Perfectly self-controlled, you never give away what you're thinking. And, if you can help it, you won't rely on anyone else to help you get your work done. You're a bit of a loner in your job, disliking being in the spotlight, and your co-workers may be a little suspicious of you. But that's just because you give them so little to go on.

You keep your personal life tightly zipped and have something of a stiffly buttoned persona. However, your composure is deceptive, for you are a compassionate, kind and caring Water sign. Workmates who have taken time to get to know you better sense your empathy and discretion, and may find themselves spilling their hearts to you. You love discovering what makes other people tick, and you're a wonderful listener. Trustworthy to your core, any gossip that finds its way to your desk will be kept strictly to yourself.

SCORPIO CAREERS

Discreet, professional and intuitive, any work where you have to research, analyze or dig deep to discover more information will suit your detective brain. You don't mess with trivialities — you get right down to business and are excellent at intuiting what's really going on with people and how they feel under the surface. Employment that involves consumer psychology, counselling or any element of negotiation suits your love of getting to the heart of what motivates people. Scorpio, along with Taurus, is one of the zodiac's financial signs. Where Taurus understands how to make money and build on it, Scorpio has a talent for merging with others in money-making ventures. You would find banking, accounting, real estate — or any position where you make a commission from other people's investments — very satisfying.

SCORPIO AT THE TOP

If you've made it to the top of your profession — and dynamic, ambitious Scorpio usually do — you'll probably have a bit of a reputation for being something of a ruthless negotiator. You never let on about what you really want until after you have it, so your business moves are often cloaked in secrecy.

There's no problem you can't solve, and your professional manner demands respect without ever asking for it. You rarely raise your voice to anyone in your charge, but there's an edge to you that suggests you might. You appear unemotional to the point of coldness, but very occasionally, and usually because of a breach of privacy or trust, you'll flip your lid. The people around you won't quite believe you're the same person.

You give away little about your own life, yet you miss nothing about what your employees get up to. They'll have to be far more devious if they believe they can pull the wool over your eyes, and you'll spot when they're on social media or pretending to work when they're actually shopping.

You don't make a big deal of minor transgressions, but you'll create a mental note of them in case they come in useful at a later date. You don't want to rock the boat unless you have to, preferring to keep your energy, and everyone else's attention, on the job at hand. Your fabled Scorpio stinger is rarely seen in the workplace, though colleagues may gossip about that one legendary time when you allegedly punched the head of marketing, and you won't say anything to dispel the myth. But more likely, if you really take a dislike to someone, you'll just completely ignore them!

Perfect Scorpio careers
- Negotiator • Spy
- Detective • Tax consultant • Police force
- Funeral director • Researcher • Psychologist
- Miner • Investment banker

SCORPIO FRIENDS AND FAMILY

You're usually self-contained enough to feel quite happy in your own company and you don't see the point of maintaining acquaintances unless there's a compelling reason. You don't need a companion on shopping trips or to gossip with over coffee. So, when you do form a new friendship, that person will probably already have a shared interest or be especially interesting to you.

You can be terrifyingly honest with your pals, and if they ask your opinion, they should be prepared to handle the answer. Some may be offended by your bluntness, but it's your authenticity that also makes your opinion so sought after. You find flattery quite suspicious, and will put your feelers out for ulterior motives, so you wouldn't dream of being the bearer of empty compliments.

Some mistake your seriousness and dislike of giving praise as unfriendly, but they'd be missing out on what having a true friend really means. When you are committed, that's it, they have your heart. You make friends for life and you will fiercely support and defend people you care about. You're just not into the conventional social niceties — things like baby showers, housewarming parties and coffee mornings. But when it really matters, you'll be there. You're a strong shoulder to cry on and offer the sincerest advice. And if your friend has royally screwed up, you won't judge, and you'll stump up the metaphorical bail money.

You might be a little antisocial at times, and you can be weirdly secretive, but you do enjoy listening to your friends' woes and are spookily able to pinpoint exactly what they're going through. Your heart is soft under all that shiny black armour, but you let people see the real you through your uncanny empathy and kindness. There's no better friend to share painful truths with and feel understood on a soul-deep level.

SCORPIO AT HOME

Scorpio homes can be a little bare looking, decidedly flounce-free and stark. You don't quite sleep on a bed of nails, but you like a sleek, shiny, sexy style — something that's easy to keep clean while being dramatic and ordered. You're not a collector and neither are you sentimental, so you don't choose to display mementos or many photographs of fuzzy moments together. Your secret treasures — erotic letters, pictures of past loves and sexy messages — lie hidden in drawers, locked boxes, laptops and deep in the attic for your eyes only.

SCORPIO PARENT

Passionate and sensitive to your child's needs, you have an almost telepathic bond with your progeny. You may be on the controlling side, suspicious of who your kid gets involved with — or when they're older, where they're going — but it comes from a deeply protective instinct. Nobody messes with your kids... apart from you, that is!

SCORPIO CHILD

Scorpio kids' intuition is uncanny. They're not frightened of your more intense emotions; in fact, they'll find them more comforting than if you try and fake being happy. Their own emotional reactions can be very dramatic, as they're sensitive to changing atmospheres. But they also respond to love and kindness with heartbreakingly touching honesty.

HEALTHY SCORPIO

Ruled by Pluto, the powerhouse planet of extremes, your metabolism is usually high. Your calm exterior masks your intensely emotional nature, which must have a healthy outlet. Otherwise, you can get tense and lose your cool.

One of the most important things you can do for your health is talk to someone about your feelings. You have such a rich and intense emotional life, but you keep things very much to yourself. If you don't feel you can express yourself to a friend or partner, going for counselling or psychotherapy will be a therapeutic

experience where you can safely bare your soul. You
rarely do half measures and can be quite obsessive about
your health — as in taking things to excessive lengths. As
the most self-controlled sign of the zodiac, you want to
master your thoughts, emotions and physical wellbeing.
You're driven, energetic and competitive, but you usually
prefer to work out on your own. Extreme sports and
adrenaline boosters such as rock climbing, skiing, cave
diving and kite surfing will help you channel repressed
or challenging feelings, relieve stress and help move any
blocked energy.

FOOD AND DRINK

Your take-it-or-leave-it attitude sees you swing from
being obsessed with one type of food to being off your
kibbles completely. You tend to enjoy foods that others
turn their nose up at — intense dark chocolate, bitter
cocktails and pungent blue cheeses. Spicy, hot, energy-
giving foods such as curries, chilli and hot-pepper sauce
give you a satisfying kick, and you'll experiment with
anything exotic and pungent or dark and delightful.

Scorpio's dark, moody, dangerous energy makes you
the zodiac's 'sex, drugs and rock'n'roll' character. This
isn't so much for the escapism — you're far too self-
aware for that — it's more in the spirit of curiosity and
experimentation. A character of extremes, you can push
things a little too far.

You may be a little obsessive about your weight and
have probably already learned from experience that

extreme or yo-yo dieting doesn't do you any good. You get a hundred percent involved with what you're doing, so you have less trouble sticking to cabbage-soup diets, ridiculously low-calorie plans or pineapple-only type fads. You can be too disciplined for a while, then ping the other way and live like King Henry VIII for a few weeks to make up for it. Finding a balance with food, drink and medicine may be a battle at times but you will master it eventually — as you do with everything!.

Scorpio's preferred places
- Shamanic quest • Sahara Desert
- Mountaineering • Caving
- Diamond mine • Brutal detox • Iceland
- Desert island • Sewer tour
- Psychological development course

SAGITTARIUS
(23 NOVEMBER — 21 DECEMBER)

You are a frank, enthusiastic and carefree Fire sign, and your astrological symbol is the archer or centaur — a mythological creature, half man, half horse. You have an impulsive and paradoxical personality, and your character represents the balancing act between the animal side of human nature and the human search for meaning.

Legend has it that you would shoot your arrow, gallop to where it landed, then shoot again — eventually covering the entire globe, delighting in every new experience your arrow would lead you to. You adore travelling and are always ready to explore new territory and meet people from different backgrounds and cultures. You live for fun and adventure, and tackle any of life's challenges with a smile on your face and a hearty belly laugh. With fortunate, gregarious Jupiter as your ruling planet, you're a popular, cheerful soul who plunges fearlessly, and sometimes a little recklessly, into the deep end of whatever life throws at you.

SHOULD YOU STAY OR SHOULD YOU GO?
Above all, you desire the freedom to explore and experience life as fully as possible, and you're at your

happiest at the beginning of a new journey, project or romance. Your initial enthusiasm and absolute belief in what you are doing propels you forwards with tremendous force. You have a rough-and-ready energy, more bluff and blunder than a thoughtful, refined approach — some may even call you clumsy! But the sheer optimism and friendly openness you apply to everything you tackle can be very refreshing.

You're quite frightened of being tied to a routine or of creating responsibilities for yourself, as you'll soon get bored and want to see what's around the corner. You sometimes get so fidgety that you'll move on without much forethought or planning. But too much change means you skate on life's surface without becoming any the wiser, which is not your aim as a person who wants to understand life's meaning on a philosophical level. One of your life's greatest lessons is learning when to stay rooted to absorb more experience, and when to shoot your arrow and gallop towards the next challenge.

JUPITER: BROAD-MINDED AND ABLE-BODIED

Your ruling planet, jovial Jupiter, is associated with luck, optimism and abundance, and assures you have plenty of confidence in your abilities. Many Sagittarius excel at sport, as you love the challenge of being told something is not possible and then proving everyone wrong.

HONESTY AND RIGHTEOUSNESS

Your craving for authenticity means you can be a little 'on the nose' when giving your opinion — which you do frequently. For you, the truth is a dish served without a coating of sugar and, you expect the people in your life to be as blunt with you as you are with them. But not everyone else wants to hear the truth so plainly. When your partner asks how she looks in that dress, you'll consider the facts and present them candidly, rather than appreciating the question as a compliment-fishing exercise.

Luckily your uncomplicated approach is appreciated by more people than it offends, as your loved ones will know exactly where they stand — and know they can be just as honest about your faults as you are about theirs... in theory. However, another one of your contradictions is that you're not as open to criticism as you are at dishing it out. As the zodiac's truth hunter, you feel you've earned the authority to be right, and you enjoy a good verbal battle with anyone who disagrees with you. It winds you up when people challenge your intelligence, because your wisdom is real and hard-won. You've studied and understood and explored, and righteously feel you have put in the work to be right.

OPTIMISTIC DAYDREAMER

You have a colourful, effusive, humorous way of communicating with people, gesticulating and bringing your stories to life, while persuading even die-hard sceptics over to your way of thinking. You are a warm, charismatic and engaging speaker and have little trouble in attracting romantic interest. An idealist to your core, you absolutely believe in the power of love and are ever optimistic that you'll find it.

You can have quite a passionate, fiery relationship with the people closest to you because you can be quite dogmatic in your beliefs. You encourage debate and are not frightened of conflict, which can be difficult for Water signs or less self-assured, more contemplative characters. Although it's often you who started the disagreement in the first place, you don't like feeling that your superior knowledge is being disrespected. Then you'll get restless, which can make your mind wander... perhaps the grass will be greener elsewhere. You never think your true love got away — you're always sure The One is just around the corner.

BIG SPENDER

Money can be something of a sore point for Sagittarius's lusty spending habits. Hating to be restricted or restrained, especially when it comes to fun, you cheerfully spend money as quickly as you make it. You tend towards making bold or even risky decisions with your finances and will probably have burned your fingers more than once when you've either gambled or invested unwisely. But again, you're a paradoxical creature, and your ruler, Jupiter, is the luckiest planet of all!

Just when you're down to your last pennies, your fortunes can change, and you're back in the black again. But as budgeting or spending wisely often entails not eating the most expensive meals, or shopping less, or cutting down on holidays, this is not going to work in tandem with your extravagant habits.

You'll probably see-saw from one extreme to the next until something just breaks. Maybe you must ask your brother or sister to help you out again, and just feel too guilty to ask for more. Perhaps you get refused a bank loan or miss a mortgage payment and get into problems with debt. There will be a point when you have to be a grown-up about money — even if you're a parent or grandparent by then!

Of course, less likely, but sometimes true for lucky Sagittarius, things can go the other way. Maybe you have a big win on the horses, land an inheritance or become a wildly successful travel blogger. But do your future self a favour and stick some of it in a bank account you can't touch — or bury your gold in the garden!

SAGITTARIUS IN LOVE

Half horse, half human, you're a creature of contradictions, striving for a balance between your animal instincts and enlightened thinking — and love can tear you in two directions. Intellectual compatibility is essential, though you're a serious epicurean and lust after more earthly pleasures, too. You value your freedom very deeply, so thinking that you may be in love with someone can bring up mixed feelings and will awaken your questioning, philosophical nature. You may initially think it's a passing fad. You'll question yourself and you might ponder what being in love actually means: whether romantic love is so different to any other kind of love; and if it isn't, why does romance scare the pants off you? Do you think you can be in love and still see other people, or take off on your own for long periods of time? Do lovers still get married these days? Do I want children? Do I want children with this person? There's a great deal to contemplate, but when it comes right down to it, you're as easily bitten by the love bug as anyone else!

EXUBERANT AND HOPEFUL

Whether initially you're drawn to a person's beautiful mind, or it's pure animal attraction, for you to be truly interested in someone romantically they have to be pretty special, because you are so deeply curious about everyone in your life. The fact that this person has your full attention is quite a feat in itself, and now you have to win them over.

You throw yourself into everything you do with the subtlety of a bulldozer, so your intended will have to be in denial not to notice your romantic overtures. You're flirtatious and warm, and you love to play the clown. Big on jokes, puns and generally playing the fool, you can be boisterous, loud and clumsy, and hard to ignore. But it's your optimism and enormous appetite for life that win the heart of whoever you have your arrow trained on. If you receive the slightest encouragement from the object of your affection, you'll gallop at speed towards them.

EPICUREAN LOVER

It may be true that only fools rush in, and as you're an idealistic daydreamer in love, your eyes may not be fully open when you first offer someone your heart. But your blind faith and good humour help you navigate most relationship ups and downs. Your optimism is infectious, and you'll soon win over even the coldest hearts. An easy-going, generous type, you want to share your whole world with your lover and experience life's adventures and challenges together. A true Epicurean, you seek pleasure in all forms and boast an enormous appetite for food, sex, laughter and fun, and you'll generously shower your partner with all of life's delights.

When everything you do is larger than life, and your hopes are cloud-high, it's only a matter of time before your rose-tinted spectacles fall from your nose and the object of so much adoration falls from their pedestal. Your Fire-sign passion is sometimes short-lived, and your wanderlust can return once things have cooled to a friendly sizzle. A cosy, comfortable kind of love isn't terribly exciting for you as a creature of such restless extremes, and you can be painfully blunt when your feelings have changed.

Most compatible love signs

LEO you're both generous, warm and
   have big hearts, Leos are one of the few
   zodiac signs who lives up to your high
   expectations.

LIBRA you're intellectually well-matched,
   sociable and fair-minded and don't shy
   away from having a heated discussion.

GEMINI witty, funny and clever,
   the pair of you never tire of talking to each
   other, whether you're gossiping about
   friends or searching for the meaning of life.

TRICKY EMOTIONS

Extremely generous in love, you expect only one thing
in return: 100% honesty. You keep your end of the
bargain by being scrupulously, painfully honest with
your partner. Your truths tend to be delivered bluntly,
with scant regard for your loved one's feelings. Unless
your partner is also a no-frills-loving Sagittarius,
you're going to bruise a few egos and may even break
a few hearts along the way. And if you're really honest,
which you are to your core, you'll have to admit that
sometimes you're just spoiling for a fight or looking
for an excuse to move on to pastures new.

Least compatible love signs

SCORPIO Scorpio's secretive nature
frustrates and scares you a little — what's so
bad or good that it can't be explored open
and honestly?

CANCER where you are reckless and brave,
Cancer is defensive and suspicious — you
can definitely teach each other something,
but romantically it's a damp squib.

VIRGO you enjoy Virgo's sharp intellect, but
they're too anxious about trivial details for
you to feel relaxed around them.

SAGITTARIUS AT WORK

Everyone needs an optimistic, cheerful, enterprising
Sagittarian in the workplace. You light up the office
with your infectious enthusiasm and willingness to
take on any challenge. Your belief in yourself, and in
the projects you're involved with, carries everyone
forward, even if you sometimes lose interest over the
less exciting aspects, such as budgeting or planning
detailed schedules.

As long as you find some value and meaning in your
role, you'll not become too restless.

Principled to the end, you'll stick up for yourself if
you feel unfairly treated, and if you're feeling unhappy

at work you might even rock the boat a little to change the direction things are going in. You actually enjoy a good verbal scrap! You're not backwards in speaking your mind, and you don't cower away from authority figures, so if your boss has annoyed you, he or she will know about it. You really dislike rules, or being told what to do, so you're bound to have had a few disagreements with employers or co-workers along the way. If you feel creatively restrained, or that your ideas are not being considered, you'll push the boundaries to see what you can get away with.

As the zodiac's intrepid explorer, you've probably tried many different careers. Your talents are broad, and you are flexible. Always optimistic and future-focused, you believe that the next job will be the best yet, even if you leave a trail of unsuccessful or incomplete career attempts behind you.

INTELLECTUAL OR SPORTY?

A contradictory character, there are usually two kinds of Sagittarius — academics, and physically sporty types. Careers that satisfy your thirst for knowledge include teaching, whether sharing skills with youngsters in school or as a lecturer, professor or expert in a particular area. You are generous with your time, and your enthusiasm and belief in what you're teaching can be very inspiring. You can make any subject sound exciting because you get to the heart of what makes it interesting. You're deeply intrigued by what drives people to accept particular ideas and reject others. Spiritual or humanitarian vocations, such as being employed as a charity aid worker, minister, counsellor or politician, would satisfy your hankering for meaningful knowledge and study.

Sports-obsessed Sagittarius are enthusiastic, encouraging coaches and trainers. You can see the bigger picture of what's ahead — and the more challenging, the better. You're full of bravado and eternally optimistic, which is ideal whether you're a team player, going it alone as a professional tennis player, or coaching a school football team.

Your punchy energy is infectious, but you rarely look before you leap, and you'll have more than your fair share of accidents and battle scars. Older Sagittarius will have learned to tone down their raucous, boisterous side, but most will admit they can still be clumsy.

ARCHER IN CHARGE

Sagittarius are happier being the boss than they are at toeing the line. Outgoing, reasonable and capable of immense vision, you are natural leadership material. You're the perfect person to be in charge of an overarching message, as you never lose sight of what it is you're trying to achieve on a grander scale.

Although impatient when bored, you never get tired of hearing our own voice, especially if you are explaining how other people ought to be doing something. You may be in charge, but you're not a strict authoritarian. Good-humoured and generous, your spending habits are often out of control, blowing ridiculous sums on making others happy rather than investing back into your company. This probably means you're an inefficient but very popular employer!

> ### Perfect Sagittarius careers
> • Travel agent • Sales person
> • Sports coach • Entrepreneur • Teacher
> • Theologian • Overseas aid worker
> • Spiritual guru • Politician • Explorer

SAGITTARIUS FRIENDS AND FAMILY

A born optimist, enthusiastic and bubbly, you love to spread a bit of happiness around your social circle. You're a particularly generous friend who enjoys lavishing attention on your pals — and you have the extravagant credit-card bills to show for it! As an outgoing, exuberant person, your social life is a big part of who you are, and you're always on hand to encourage and entertain.

You do fun like no other zodiac sign, organizing parties, adventures and amusing events to keep everyone together and smiling. You're something of a practical joker and lighten even the gloomiest days with your wit and clowning. But when someone close to you is feeling down, you know exactly what to say. For all your love of silliness, you do offer disarmingly profound advice.

The only time you might rub your pals up the wrong way is by refusing to back down in an argument, or through your 'honesty at all costs' policy. When you believe you are right about something there is no shifting you. You can also be terribly blunt. Honesty is important, but you can be more forthright than thoughtful in giving your opinion, which others may take as criticism and find quite hurtful. A little diplomacy will help you open a more tolerant and broad-minded discussion, which is really what you want to happen, rather than being shut down by aggrieved friends the second you start talking about a contentious issue.

You also exhibit something of a double standard in your honesty. You're scrupulous when it comes to speaking your truth and hearing others speaking theirs. But if you're entertaining friends with a ripping yarn, you'll think nothing of wildly embellishing or exaggerating your tale for entertainment value. Life is never dull when you're around, and in many ways your friends are the most important people in your life, so you will go over and beyond what it takes to make them happy.

SAGITTARIUS AT HOME

Not naturally a homebody, you're always thinking of where to go next, so wherever you choose to lay your hat may have a temporary feel. You are happiest outdoors, in nature, so naturally you'll feel more at home if plants and plenty of light are part of your decor. Ideally, you'd have large windows you can gaze out of, daydreaming of your next adventure. You have a 'bigger is better' opinion on home furnishings, and your abode may be filled with maps, spiritual figurines and cultural mementos (some would say clutter!) from your many trips. Your taste is loud, proud and over-the-top, with a love of bold patterns and wild colour schemes.

SAGITTARIUS PARENT

You're a superb teacher and will naturally pass your openness and curiosity about life on to your children. Scouting, travelling and enjoying nature will see you at your best; you'll encourage any sporting abilities, and instil a healthy sense of competitiveness and a fearless approach to challenges.

SAGITTARIUS CHILD

Sagittarian kids love their freedom. They have adventurous spirits and will love to explore. They'll push against any rules, but when they're older and you can reason with them, they'll listen to your sound judgment. Sagittarius are the least money-savvy sign of the zodiac, so the earlier you can teach your child about money management, the better.

HEALTHY SAGITTARIUS

Sagittarius has something of a dual nature, with people of the sign falling into either the active, physical, horse side or the intellectual, pondering, human half of the archer/centaur. Occasionally people do cross over into both territories, but you'll probably know instinctively which side you favour.

If you're a sporty, speedy, gym-loving Sagittarius, you'll be robust, energetic and competitive. Athletics and team games provide a natural outlet to burn off some of that excess Fire-sign spirit. Hiking, rock climbing and sailing all appeal to your hale and hearty love for outdoor travel, and should prove exciting enough to hold your attention. You're naturally speedy, love a challenge and have complete faith in your abilities. An excellent teacher, you are an inspiring coach and role model, and enjoy encouraging others to achieve their personal best.

If you're more of a thoughtful type of Sagittarian, who prefers your travel to be more mental than physical, you'll be an avid reader, with an insatiable curiosity about the people around you. But you're probably less interested in physical exercise. Luckily, almost all Sagittarians find walking therapeutic, as it stimulates the mind and the body, soothes your restlessness and satisfies your curiosity to see what's around the next corner.

FOOD AND DRINK

Your enormous appetite for life extends to food and drink, which you enjoy in large quantities. Your ruling planet, Jupiter, is associated with expansion and taking things too far, so you'll find it tricky not to overindulge in the good things. Your ruler, Jupiter, isn't terribly discriminating in its tastes; he just wants to expand what is on offer. You're a quantity rather than quality person, a supermarket shopper rather than a specialist grocer — or even better, both! Imagine a medieval banquet with an enormous table creaking with ample portions of meat, jellies, rich puddings, fruit, wine and beer — that's your kind of dinner!

As a party-loving creature of excess, you loathe limiting yourself when you're having a good time, and of course that will probably include enjoying a few beers, glasses of wine and strong cocktails. You can drink most other zodiac signs under the table, but you'll probably have already learned the hard way that some excesses are more of a headache than others!

NO LIMITS

Of course, all this overindulgence and love of rich foods leads to steady weight gain, and if you're not the sporty Sagittarian type you'll have a propensity to become a little girthy. Sagittarians aren't usually lithe and lean, and unless you're very athletic, you'll have a jovial Jupiter rotundity to your body. Watching your weight does not come naturally, as you rebel against any form of restraint and can be quite undisciplined when it comes to sticking to rules around food.

Luckily, most restless Fire signs move around so much and have such a high metabolism that you'll burn up plenty of calories being just plain fidgety. And that big brain of yours uses almost as much energy as half an hour on a treadmill.

Sagittarius's preferred places
• Zimbabwe walking safari • Pompeii
• Whale spotting • Madagascar
• Outer Mongolia • Cattle ranching
• Polynesia • New Zealand
• Siberia • Inca trek

CAPRICORN
(22 DECEMBER — 20 JANUARY)

Y ou are a realistic, practical and hard-working person — the most ambitious character in the zodiac. The astrological symbol for Capricorn is the Goat, sometimes depicted as a mythical sea goat. The Goat represents your patient determination to scale great heights and reach the pinnacle in all your endeavours. You have lofty goals and the intelligence and diligence to achieve them. As an Earth sign, you are pragmatic and stoical, firmly rooted in the tangible world, and you trust in what you can see, touch and build. Responsible, structure-loving Saturn is your ruling planet, which gives you a realistic, if slightly cynical, outlook on life. You expect to work very hard to achieve success, and respect others who have set a good example.

OLD HEAD, YOUNG SHOULDERS

Capricorns tend to start life with an old head on young shoulders and lighten up as they age. Stern Saturn often presents Capricorns with challenges early in life, and you may have had to shoulder extra responsibilities or encountered limiting circumstances. The humbler your beginnings, the greater your determination to overcome any challenges on the rocky road up the mountain. And in dealing with character-forming situations so young, you learned to become self-reliant. You are confident in your ability to succeed, but Saturn probably left you with a few niggly self-esteem issues or a feeling of insecurity, which you'll be determined to mask by flinging yourself into a constant state of refinement and improvement.

On top of setting your sights very high in your career, you're also something of a social climber, and enjoy rubbing shoulders with people who have 'made it' in your eyes. Some will be dear friends, but you're probably guilty of indulging in a spot of name-dropping, hoping you'll appear a little more impressive. You're not a loud or ostentatious person, but you want to be respected for your achievements, because secretly you may feel like you're an imposter who just got lucky.

You're not always the fastest to learn new skills, but you have legendary stamina and patience. Whereas others give up when the going gets rough, you keep slowly but surely ploughing through until you have what you want in your sights. Your burdens become lighter as you get older — or perhaps it's your attitude that changes, as you learn not to be so hard on yourself. Saturn has set you an intimidating set of standards to live by, but he has also endowed you with the organizational skills, prudence and self-discipline to shine. As you gain confidence, you brighten with every achievement, mellowing with age as a cheerier, more carefree you emerges over time.

CLEVER WITH MONEY

As a sensible, accumulative Earth sign, you're excellent with money. You're not a frivolous spender. With a mature head on your shoulders, you're not about to waste the money you put so much time and energy into creating. One of the main reasons you're such a financial whizz is that you know when to act. You don't procrastinate, and you don't make excuses — you have a plan and you stick to it. It might not be rocket science, but surprisingly few people have the common sense or discipline to plough through tasks in quite the same way.

You're a saver and a prudent investor, clever at maths, facts and figures — and careers in finance will be an attractive option. You're a cool operator and a thoughtful strategist, and if you don't know how something works, you'll learn! Not impulsive by nature, you spend your money wisely, and you can spot the value in other people's skills and talents. With an eye for things that stand the test of time, Capricorns make excellent art and antique dealers, estate agents and jewellers. Yours isn't a boom-or-bust zodiac sign, and you'll make your fortune slowly, over a long period of time. Even financially embarrassed Capricorns will have a business plan or two carefully tucked away, waiting for the right moment.

LONELY AT THE TOP

Authoritative Saturn ensures you feel comfortable at the helm in any business. Your drive, knowledge and sheer hard work eventually propel you to the top of your game, and as you've been headed up that mountain most of your life, it's naturally where you feel most confident and secure. Whether you find yourself as a CEO, the head of a small company or a self-made entrepreneur, you are happy being the person accountable for making all the important or final decisions.

Not everyone wishes to be tethered to their job, or cares as much about their public persona, and it can get lonely up there. You'll have made many acquaintances and enjoy a plethora of colleagues and co-workers, so romance may have taken something of a back seat while you concentrated on your career. But family is extremely important to you, and you have a strong sense of duty. You wouldn't hesitate to give up your career completely if you had to look after an elderly parent, and your loyalty to your roots would see you stick with a family business to make it a success, even if you'd secretly have preferred to try something different.

FUNNY FEELINGS

Nobody could accuse you of coming across as too gushy! Capricorns usually have a tight rein on their emotions, or are uncomfortable expressing their more complicated feelings. For all your polished exterior, you're not quite at ease with your inner world, but again, you tend to form an easier relationship with your emotions as you get older. If you don't have many Fire or Water signs in your birth chart, having a Saturn Sun

Most compatible love signs

CANCER You share important values with your opposite sign, Cancer. You're both conscientious and cautious, and can make heaps of money together.

SCORPIO You're both quite reticent to show how you really feel, but there are fireworks when you do!

TAURUS Loyal, steady and determined, you feel safe with Taurus, and these comfort-loving characters will help you relax and smell the flowers along the way.

sign can make you more apt to analyze your thoughts or feelings instead of allowing yourself to feel sad, angry, jealous or even joyful.

As you are such a perfectionist, you should guard against becoming caught up in chasing a particular dream or ambition to the exclusion of everything else, because if things don't work out as planned, Saturn can make you be very hard on yourself. It's vitally important you don't get sucked into a negative spiral, as you'll probably dwell far too long on what you could have done to improve things — even if it no longer matters. Use pragmatic Saturn to your advantage, to allow yourself to see that you did your best — and employ your wonderfully dry sense of

Least compatible love signs

SAGITTARIUS You're quite suspicious of anyone who seems recklessly jolly for no apparent reason.

ARIES They're quite attractive for a while with their big ideas and passions, but they don't have the stamina or vision to back up anything they say.

GEMINI You like tradition; Gemini is faddish. You have serious life goals; they're all chitchat. You don't have time for this!

humour to help you loosen up a little and enjoy life to its fullest.

CAPRICORN IN LOVE

Nobody can accuse you of wearing rose-tinted spectacles when it comes to love and romance. As one of the most practical Earth signs in the zodiac, you're not about to leap up and down proclaiming your affections from the rooftops — at least not until you've thoroughly checked their reputation and background on social media, and found out if they have a car and what their future plans involve. You do have a slightly unfair reputation for being too status-conscious when it comes to choosing a partner, but that's just because you know there's no point in being with someone who doesn't share similar aspirations.

It's not that you don't want to be in love, it's just that you're the least likely sign of the zodiac to be blinded by it. You long to meet someone you can cherish and share your life with, and as you're deeply attractive, wise, funny and refined, you won't have trouble attracting the real thing. But Saturn made you a realist, and he probably taught you quite early in life to keep your true feelings private until you are sure it's safe to reveal them — and this can take time. You may even put off looking for a relationship until you're happy that your career is on the right track, as you're wise enough to consider how much time you would be able to commit to a serious relationship when you're still trying to establish yourself in your chosen field.

When you do meet someone suitable, you don't treat it lightly because you know it could be a lifetime's commitment. You'll take things seriously, calmly and quite slowly so you can be sure they can be trusted with your surprisingly fragile heart. Then when you do commit, you're definitely all in — mind, body and soul. When you trust another enough to let your guard down, they'll be delighted to see a side of you that the rest of the word rarely does: loving, gentle and passionate, with a wickedly deadpan sense of humour.

EVERYTHING'S PERFECT

Your Saturn work ethic also applies to relationships. You don't expect even the most wonderful love affairs to be sunshine and rainbows. You understand that nobody is perfect, and you'll include your own flaws and idiosyncrasies in that equation. The best partnerships take effort, and unless you have a predominance of flighty Air of reckless Fire signs in your chart, you will be devoted to making the commitment work. Naturally you'll enjoy setting goals for yourself as a couple — perhaps even working hard to set up a business together.

A traditionalist at heart, you'll likely adopt the conventional model for love and romance and apply your high Capricorn standards. You'll choose a stable, albeit rather formal approach with engagement, setting up an impressive home together — and children will be discussed at the appropriate time. Your relationship may appear a little austere to people who don't know you, but your friends and loved ones will see a completely different side. Although you are always keen to project a grandiose vision of your life together, when it's just you two you drop the stiff formalities and allow yourself to be playful and vulnerable.

TRICKY EMOTIONS

The initial exciting stages of romance can be a little overwhelming for your usual cool, calm and collected persona, and you're actually far more comfortable when things settle down. But this can be a tougher time for your partner, who may feel concerned that you're withdrawing your more spontaneous emotions. This is probably not a conscious decision, and is just a sign that you're relaxed enough to be yourself. But you can't expect your partner to be psychic, so try not to let your practical side override or obscure your fun-loving, affectionate nature. Your ruler, Saturn, may be something of a 'glass half empty' type of ruling planet, but you would do well to remember that once the hard work is done, you're allowed to enjoy yourself!

CAPRICORN AT WORK

You are a born business mastermind — the hardest worker in the zodiac. And if you haven't already achieved something prestigious or impressive, you'll be slowly working your way towards it. After all, reaching the top is what goat people naturally want to do. You size up any challenges in your way with a cool head, and learn the skills you need on the steep slope to the top of the mountain.

You're super-practical and organized, and will probably have a strict plan of action. As one of the most disciplined people around, you can be a little harsh on yourself if you feel you've wasted an opportunity or spent too much time on something frivolous, like consuming a meal in your lunch hour... or having a loo break.

EMPLOYEE OF THE YEAR

As an employee, you're the first person to switch the light on in the office and are often the last to leave. You're trusted with extra-heavy workloads because you're known as a steady pair of hands: methodical, conscientious and reliable. You don't quibble, and you'll never tell your boss that something can't be done; you'll find a way, even if it means working overtime or learning a whole new set of skills.

You always have half an eye on the top job, but totally respect the hard work and solid effort it takes to get there. As a disciplined Saturn-ruled person, you wouldn't feel comfortable in a position you felt was handed to you on a plate. You need to feel you've earned your right to be there.

You're generally the quiet, conservatively dressed, well-spoken person who's careful with money. You can be trusted to look after anything from the kitty for the tea and biscuits to the economy of a large country. You're that rare breed that's gifted at maths and enjoys accounts, so you find working out the company tax bill quite satisfying — and even feel a twinge of pleasure in paying it.

Whereas other zodiac signs would shrug it off pretty fast, if you make a mistake at work you'll feel miserable, as so much of your self-esteem is wrapped up with your job. But for the same reason, you'll learn from every misstep and vow never to make the same error twice.

You have the drive and ambition to be a self-made entrepreneur, as you're not easily discouraged, and your decision to set up your own business will be based on facts and meticulous research. You also have the patience and appreciation of structure to draw you to a career in accountancy or banking. Goal-oriented, you would enjoy setting regular targets for anyone in your team, whether you work for a large corporation or a small, niche business.

GOAT AT THE TOP

If you're a Capricorn boss, you're right where you ought to be! A high achiever, you belong to the corporate world, and your patience and exceptional problem-solving skills mean you have the potential to be one of the most efficient and committed professionals in the workforce. You favour traditional methods and are a bit suspicious of shortcuts. Saturn may make you feel weighed down with responsibility, and you're generally quiet about your considerable achievements. However, you will allow yourself a few aspirational status symbols: a sedate but expensive company car and parking space and an imposing desk or office are all par for the course.

Firm but fair, you're a decent boss who rewards loyalty and a job well done. But if anyone tries to pull the wool over your eyes you'll not be amused. People need to be honest, put in the hours and, above all, show you the same respect you'd have for a person in your position. Although you're the ultimate professional, and can be a little shy or formal, when you feel comfortable, your cynical, dry sense of humour comes out to play, surprising anyone who doesn't know you well. But you have to earn that rare privilege with a Capricorn boss.

CAPRICORN FRIENDS AND FAMILY

You're a loyal friend, reliable and constant, and you see it as your duty to look after the people who have been in your life for a long time. Old friends feel like family to you, and with sage old Saturn, the Lord of Time, as your ruling planet, you'll naturally get on with people from different generations. You're a realist at heart and fully accept that you won't be young forever, which gives you an unusually deep respect for older people's knowledge and wisdom.

You also appreciate having a good old-fashioned moan with friends, sharing your work woes, having a gripe about the government and generally lamenting the state of the world with someone who agrees with you. You're a very therapeutic person in this respect, as everyone needs a friend who they can have a jolly good grumble with and set the world to rights.

DEADPAN HUMOUR

You also deeply appreciate people who can bring you out of a gloomy mood or make you forget about work entirely. Your ruler, Saturn, might not be the cheeriest of planets, but he's taught you to enjoy a healthy dose of well-observed sarcasm. You'll have at least one friend with a droll sense of humour, and the pair of you will

Perfect Capricorn careers
- Politician • Accountant
- Legal secretary • Estate agent
- Town planner • Mortgage advisor
- Lecturer • Entrepreneur
- Business analyst • Architect

probably have your own secret language and keep each other in stitches.

You are extremely self-reliant and trust yourself first and foremost — so it can be tough sharing fears or personal problems with others. You rarely admit to any insecurities and are a bit worried that others will think you unworthy of your success, but usually the opposite is true. When you let friends and loved ones in, you'll discover that, rather than judging you, they'll be touched that you let down your guard to reveal your true self. When you feel that the real you is valued and accepted, warts and all, you will feel less pessimistic.

A good old-fashioned night out on the town watching a comedian, or an evening at the movies with friends, will all give you a break from being the one in charge, and will make you realize that the world keeps on turning, even if you're not there to supervise.

CAPRICORN AT HOME

Always striving to attain the best life can offer, regardless of your background or family circumstances, you want the best for your loved ones, so you're usually the person in charge at home as well as in the office. Whether you have your own family or not, you'll work hard to secure a home base where you can shed the weight of the world from your shoulders and relax. Tasteful but slightly austere, your home ambience reflects your deep sense of connection with the past. Grandiose antique furniture, elegant bookcases, classical decor and cool retro pieces reflect your excellent and refined taste.

CAPRICORN PARENT

You want respect from your children and have an authoritative, slightly aloof manner. You'll encourage any talents or skills and will happily support musical or creative interests. Having fun with your kids is vitally important so that they see your lighter side as well as the serious, career-oriented person.

CAPRICORN CHILD

Capricorn kids often seem older than their years and need to learn to relax and be curious about the world. These earnest boys and girls crave approval and should be praised for just being themselves, as well as being encouraged for their achievements.

HEALTHY CAPRICORN

You're blessed with a robust constitution and have the self-discipline to stick to an exercise regime that gets you the results you want. Even the most intimidating fitness challenges don't scare you off as long as you have the space and time to work incrementally towards mastering your goal. As Capricorn is the sign of the Goat, climbing will be an obvious choice, but any form of exercise where you work steadily towards success works best. You have the stamina for long-distance running and the grace and poise to be an elegant ice skater or gymnast. If you're very shy, as Capricorns tend to be, attending a regular gym class with others means you'll break through some anxieties.

FOOD AND DRINK

You have bags of Saturnian self-control when it comes to food and nutrition, and find it easier than most to adapt to healthy eating habits. When you're in the zone, you eat regularly, stick to nutritious options and don't find it too hard to cut back on calories if you need to. But if you're overworking, food can be forgotten, and you'll find yourself relying on 24-hour takeaways or living on caffeine and energy drinks. This might inject you with the temporary burst of energy you need to complete your tax return, but you'll burn out and feel even more exhausted in the long run. Getting plenty of rest is crucial for stressed-out Capricorns, as lack of downtime can see you lying awake at night thinking about your work when you ought to be fast asleep.

BEING KIND TO YOURSELF

You want to be the best at whatever you are doing, and Saturn can be a hard taskmaster. But beware that you are not pushing yourself too far with exercise, as overdoing it can put pressure on your bones — which can be a weak point. If you're going through a particularly busy or difficult time at work, you might neglect your gym membership or not have time to exercise at all. But getting enough fresh air and natural daylight, and feeling connected with the ground, is vital for Earth signs to stay healthy and vibrant.

Sleep is critical, and meditation and relaxation methods will help you unwind and focus on something other than work. You, more than anyone else, need to actively make time to be kind to yourself, as you find it easy to be self-critical if you feel you're not getting enough done, or are dissatisfied with your efforts. When you appreciate yourself a little more, you'll find that you're actually one of the few zodiac signs who looks healthier as they age — and the most likely sign to enjoy a sprightly retirement.

Capricorn's preferred places
• The Ritz • Antique shops • Pompeii
• British Museum • St Petersburg • The ballet
• Orient Express • Danube cruise
• Machu Picchu • Florence

AQUARIUS
(21 JANUARY — 19 FEBRUARY)

You are a friendly, inventive, erratic person — the zodiac's nonconformist. The astrological symbol for Aquarius is the Water Carrier, usually depicted as a man pouring water from a large vessel. This connection with water has many thinking Aquarius is a Water sign, but it is not. You're a charismatic, idealistic Air sign, and you spend more time in your head than any other sign of the zodiac.

The symbol for your ruling planet, future-focused Uranus, is two wavy lines — which again might look like water, but it actually depicts electricity. You're often described as having an exciting, inventive and volatile personality.

Uranus is the planet of sudden change, connected with rebellion, progression and genius technological breakthroughs. Uranus rules over technology, novelty and ingenuity and, in a birth chart, its position represents originality, personal freedom, excitement and surprises.

You're a reformer at heart. You look at humanity's customs, traditions and politics and want to change what's not working to create a brighter vision of society — one that's more tolerant and diverse. Your mission is to raise the planet's consciousness by bringing the world's groups and organizations together for the common good.

It can be frustrating for you that most Aquarians are so ahead of their time, that people either ignore, or are not ready to take on, your brilliant ideas. What you think makes sense now will be how the rest of us see it in 10 years. The same goes for your quirky fashion choices and contrary opinions.

CURIOUSLY OBSESSIVE

You are intensely curious about how things work, which makes you a gifted researcher, scientist or inventor. You have an erratic style and can mentally juggle many different thoughts at once. But when you're really interested in someone or something, you're compelled to take it apart, analyze all the different components and put them back together yourself... with a few improvements.

Fascinated by mysteries and esoteric philosophy, subjects such as astrology, ancient religions, conspiracy theories, and life in other dimensions or faraway galaxies inspire and excite you. You're known for your offbeat taste and style. If everyone else is getting interested in something, you'll have done it years ago and published a thesis on it. You are tech-savvy, quite obsessed with gadgets and the internet. You probably taught yourself how to program your computer, and you're the first one to know about the latest technological breakthroughs and developments via your friendly network of fellow techie geeks.

Most Aquarians are surgically attached to their phones, and social media would collapse without you as it combines your favourite things: communication with large groups of people and technology. You can get sucked into internet rabbit holes for days without sleeping or eating properly. Your brain doesn't get tired; if anything, your energy and excitement build the more information you feed it.

FRIENDLY INFATUATIONS

Your obsessions also apply to people, which can get you into some awkward situations. If someone finds themselves the object of your curiosity, you'll want to know exactly what makes them tick — right down to the nitty gritty — and you can be quite blunt and sometimes a little shocking in your questions. For example, that attractive person you bump into now and then, the musician who lives on a boat... you'll wonder how they make enough money to pay rent. Perhaps they bought the boat outright... How much are boats these days? How do they cope in the winter... and does the drum-playing bring in much cash? Where do they busk? Once you have assembled all the facts, you'll examine your chosen target's personal and psychological explanations and reasoning. If by then the person under your microscope isn't too freaked out, they may suspect you have a bit of a crush. And you do! But it's not the sort they suspect.

You're one of the world's friendliest people, but you can be a little detached from your emotions, and this disconnect can cause misunderstandings. Your otherworldly qualities can make you a very glamorous and attractive person, which means that sometimes people you're interested in will get their romantic hopes up. But once you find out everything there is to know about a person, you can become a little disappointed that the mystery wasn't as exciting as you hoped. You might then feel a little embarrassed, or explain that you were just being friendly, which could be a bit hurtful for the other party, who is no longer the centre of your world. But by then you're gone, lured away by the intense attraction of your new obsession.

TEAM AQUARIUS

One of your contradictions and challenging life lessons is that although you see yourself very much as an independent and unique individual, you love being part of a collective. You feel a sense of family belonging in large groups, whether you're sports fans, members of a social-media group, a political protest organization or a cosplay group at a sci-fi convention. You long to lose your sense of identity in a group, yet you can be peculiarly lonely. Romantic relationships can bring up difficult challenges, as you demand the freedom to explore the world in your own way and don't want to compromise. Ideally, you'll find a partner who will share some of your interests, and who will at least be a member of the groups and clubs you hold so dear. Mutual passions would make your life together easier, as sacrificing your time or interests will not be easy for you.

BRILLIANT OR DELUDED?

Sometimes you're so ahead of the game that others stop trying to keep up with your avant-garde thinking or accuse you of plucking ideas from thin air. You can appear distant or distracted and, because you don't connect with people on an emotional level, some may think you've lost the plot or are out of touch. But they're mistaken. You're sharp as nails, perhaps even more so when you're concentrating on something interesting. Always analyzing, your intellectual creativity is drawn from invisible sources that you're probably not even fully conscious of.

You make complete sense to yourself, but if you use that electric mind of yours to read your friends', colleagues' or partner's thoughts, you'll see that sometimes they think you're talking a different language. It may pay off to slow down your thought process just a notch so you can communicate more effectively when you need to.

UNEXPECTEDLY STUBBORN

Nobody tells you what to do or think, but if anyone does try to control you, you'll quite calmly do the opposite of what is expected of you. It's just not in your nature to toe the line or stick to anyone else's formula. You are often the catalyst that forces other people to change their ways, and for someone who delights in upsetting the applecart, you're actually rather stubborn. Once you have decided that you're right about something, there is simply no other explanation available. You're extremely clever, and you may even be in touch with a higher intelligence that not everyone else has access to. But regardless of how you reach your decisions, you believe in your own supreme, sometimes irrational logic. This is another intriguing Aquarian character contradiction, because you're so keen to see change in society, and are completely open-minded about progress. But when it comes to your own personal behaviour, you'll not budge.

AQUARIUS IN LOVE

You're the zodiac's humanitarian, everyone's friend, and you're deeply curious about others. If you're on a date with someone interesting, you often flatter them into thinking you're really interested in them because you ask so many questions. You go into so much detail about their likes, dislikes and what they had for breakfast that morning that the other person can be a little bowled over. They could be forgiven for thinking that they might be rather special. And, of course, you think they're rather wonderful, too... but you're probably just as interested in their mother, or the guy with the weird hat on the other table, or the woman playing the piano in the corner of the restaurant.

Not everyone is as attentive or curious as you, without hoping that things might progress in a romantic kind of way. And your ardent curiosity can inadvertently lead some hopeful people to think they're in with a chance. This can come as something of a surprise to you.

DETACHED AND UNSELFISH

You love in a gentle, eternally friendly way, and have an almost scientific interest in the people around you. But you're a bit out of your depth when it comes to physical feelings such as lust, jealousy or passion. As a lofty Air sign, you live in your big, crazy, colourful mind, and go where your eternal curiosity leads you. You're a free spirit, and often when you've discovered everything about the person you're scrutinizing, your attention is grabbed by someone, or something, else. Uranus has you firmly focused on the future, so you can hop from an obsession with one person to the next without much trouble, and can find it baffling when others feel hurt by your fickleness.

Unless you have a few Fire or Earth signs in your chart, you don't really get jealous or possessive over people you care about — and you don't understand when you've aroused such passions in others. You're unselfish and detached in your affections, thinking everyone is unique in some way, so it's rare for you to feel overtaken by an attraction to one person in particular. But it does happen.

LOVE VERSUS LOGIC

You're delightfully cool and glamorous, and exude an air of mystery, which means you're not short of admirers. But for you to get really hooked on someone they'll probably have an intriguing, rather aloof air. When you do meet someone who has you entranced, you may be as giddy as a teenager in the first flush of romance, walking along the street bumping into lamp posts. You'll be excited and a little disturbed that you've found someone who is different to everyone else. But it won't be long before you start analyzing what it all really means.

You're a supremely logical creature, and love can be a tricky concept for you to get your head around. You think love is just love; you believe in caring for humanity as group and looking out for each other as a collective. When one person means everything to you, you'll be perplexed but excited; after all, it's a new experience that you will be happy to explore. But you'll wonder what is expected of you in return. Will you have to give up your freedom? Can you commit to one person forever? And so the analyzing begins...

INDEPENDENCE AND COMPROMISE

You're an oddball, Aquarius. You love the weirdest ideas and freely travel the globe pursuing them. You genuinely don't expect other people to move to a Japanese commune, believe in aliens or come to live with you in your converted ambulance — but you're not about to give up any of your strange beliefs or peculiar lifestyle to settle down in a semi-detached house and have a family. That's far too predictable for you, unless you find a workable compromise.

Your partner knew what you were like before you committed yourself to one another, so they should already have accepted your need for freedom and independence. If they've stuck with you through your stint as a water-slide tester or an international trampolinist, they'll probably already love this about

Most compatible love signs

LIBRA Gentle, harmonious, romantic Libra can teach you how to love without throwing any awkward emotional tantrums.

LEO You're in awe of Leo's willingness to please others and secretly think they know something you don't.

AQUARIUS You're unique — they're unique. You both don't mind sleeping on futons; you plan to build a dwelling out of old car doors and breed iguanas.

Least compatible love signs

TAURUS Taurus like to know what they're having for dinner tonight. But the last time you ate a regular meal, you were in prison!

SCORPIO You're very curious about Scorpio, because you know they're hiding something. But you're afraid to find out what it is!

CANCER You can't always tell what you did to upset Cancer, but you know it must have been really bad.

you, and won't expect you to attend church every Sunday or sit on the couch every night... though you may well decide to try either of these for a while, just to prove them wrong!

TRICKY EMOTIONS

You're often embarrassed by emotions — you own and others' — and you'll do your best to keep yours hidden. You tend to dissociate from unpleasant feelings like jealousy, anger, aggression or neediness. But when your logical mind accepts that having to deal with all emotions — the dark ones and the beautiful ones — is what makes us human, you'll find there's a nobleness in reasoning that you're only human too.

AQUARIUS AT WORK

It may take you a while before you find a career that will keep you interested. You'll happily investigate, experiment and explore while you're young, finding a position that doesn't make you want to staple your fingers to a desk out of boredom. You'll have no trouble being offered work, because although your unconventional approach may put some people off initially, they soon discover that you're an eccentric little goldmine.

Your Uranus-ruled mind would be wasted in a mundane or routine job, unless you have a large circle of friends there. You thrive in teams and might stick around in a place where you like the people, or the ethos is right. You're generous with your talents, and you'll happily volunteer your skills in unpaid work for a progressive or exciting organization.

You're something of an enigma to your colleagues — cool-headed and distant one minute and intensely focused and engaged the next. You can be quite pig-headed when you've made up your mind about something too, quite rigidly sticking to your (often outlandish) opinions and expecting others to be on board. Sometimes you can be accused of saying something outrageous just to rock the boat, and being told 'things have always been done this way' brings you out in a rash.

UNCONVENTIONAL GENIUS

You have something of an 'absent-minded-professor' reputation at work. You come up with genius money-making ideas while you're on your tea break, but have half an eye on the cricket score in important meetings. It's not that you don't follow rules to be difficult, or shock people deliberately, it's just that your mind is doing something far more interesting and absorbing than remembering when to eat lunch or discovering you're not meant to bring your cat to work. You already know how to run cars on water, teleport to different planets and cure the common cold — but you got so caught up in your next thought that you forgot to tell anyone about it.

You enjoy being in an office because even though you care not a jot for social conventions, you're a particularly friendly person, and your colleagues will think you're a breath of fresh air. When everyone else is wearing smart suits and shiny shoes, you'll be in flip-flops with red braces and a deerstalker hat. You don't really do anything when it's meant to be done, but somehow what you come up with on the train to work is often as good as what your co-workers can produce in a week.

How you actually got the job will be steeped in legend, as you often end up working in different organizations without having formally applied for a position. You may call up a CEO about an idea you've had only to be accused of time-wasting, then offered a job when they discover your invention could save them a ton of money.

AQUARIAN IN CHARGE

You might be the boss, but your unconventional approach to work means you'll probably not look or act like one. You're actually not that comfortable working alone and are more at ease networking in large groups. You don't want to feel like there's a barrier between you and your colleagues — you want to be amongst them, listening to their ideas and finding out about their lives. You're not a harsh or strict boss, but you expect them to keep up with you mentally.

You want to make society a better place and you're not afraid to think outside the box — although some of it is so ahead of time it needs to go back into the box until the rest of the world is ready! You have a radar for what people are about to do and how to improve people's lives with your original solutions. You're not that interested in rank and hierarchy in your job, and you genuinely don't care what other people think of you. It's never about the money or the status for Aquarius — it's about changing society, ripping up old traditions and customs that are no longer working and replacing them with brilliant new ideas that will revolutionize the planet.

Perfect Aquarius careers
• Scientist • Politician • Professor
• Inventor • Astrologer • Engineer
• Computer programmer
• Air-traffic controller
• Social-enterprise professional
• Alternative therapist

AQUARIUS FRIENDS AND FAMILY

Companionship and friendliness are your thing, Aquarius; it's your natural state of being. You're usually a key part of any community, looking out for everyone around you. Shared interests give you a sense of humanitarian purpose, so you'll be a well-known face at local sports clubs, a volunteer at the homeless shelter and a much-loved character in the local pub.

You'll likely be the organizer of many different clubs and groups for your local area on social media, and your idiosyncratic ideas and unorthodox fashion sensibilities mean everyone knows your face. Sometimes you're the person pushing the dog around in the pram, or you'll be the proud owner of the garden full of ceramic frogs. You'll either have a vintage three-wheeler Reliant Robin parked on your drive, or a state-of-the-art, eco-friendly, electric Tesla.

INDEPENDENT FREE SPIRIT

Transfixed by other people's lives and interests, you delight in good old-fashioned gossip, but you rarely let hearsay cloud your opinion of anyone — if anything, a dodgy reputation just makes people more interesting to you. It's an Aquarius contradiction that although you are strongly drawn to be part of a team, group or society, you're actually a very private person.

You don't usually have intimate friendships with people on a one-to-one basis, perhaps fearing that you may become too responsible for them or not wanting to become too entangled in others' lives. Above everything else, you require the freedom to act as you please, unimpeded by other people's decisions.

But you are such a wonderful friend to everyone and think nothing of helping in any practical way possible to make a difference. You, however, can find it difficult to ask for help when you need it. If you do need assistance, you'll be knocked sideways by the kindness of loved ones — everyone from your brother to the postman would willingly pitch in to lend you a hand. Perhaps if you slowed down a little, you'd see how appreciated you are.

AQUARIUS AT HOME

Not bound by traditional gender roles, or indeed any conventions, your home may reflect your love of tech and modern taste. Your ideal pad would be ultra-futuristic and minimalist — all polished steel, glass, large windows and robots to help you vacuum. In reality, however, your home environment likely resembles your scattered mind, filled with discarded machines and computers waiting for you to fix them.

You're also one of the most environmentally friendly signs of the zodiac, a purposeful recycler who assigns every piece of rubbish an inventive new lease of life as building material, furniture, plant pot or hammock.

AQUARIUS PARENT

Before they learn to walk properly, your kids will probably understand how to rewire a plug and change a light bulb. And they'll certainly know their way around a computer. Your brilliant and eccentric imagination delights your children, whose minds you love to keep alert and curious. You keep your little ones occupied with lively conversation and a plentiful supply of books and puzzles. You'll also be a keen participant in video games and online learning.

AQUARIUS CHILD

Aquarius children enjoy being surrounded by other youngsters, as their curiosity about others is how they do most of their learning. They'll feel very much at home when involved with club or group activities such as Scouts, Brownies and sport teams. But they are also highly academic, with scientific minds; they soak up technical knowledge like little electric sponges.

HEALTHY AQUARIUS

As a mentally focused Air sign, sometimes you get so caught up in what you're doing that you're genuinely surprised that your body exists at all, never mind that it's complaining it's hungry, or stiff from sitting in the same position. It can be hard for you to get really motivated about moving your body because it can take you away from what you're really interested in.

With inventive, unpredictable Uranus as your ruling planet, your energy levels are usually high, but they can also be erratic. Long nights staring at your computer, or using all your energy trying to solve a scientific puzzle, could leave you feeling frazzled. Sometimes your body appears to just switch itself off for a quick reset... more commonly known to the other zodiac signs as 'sleep'.

Exercise isn't something you like to schedule or think of as routine. You get bored with any repetitive physical movement — and going to the gym at the same time every day won't appeal much. But as an extroverted, social sign of the zodiac, being around others lifts your spirits and fills you with energy — so team sports and busy classes will prove more fulfilling. A bit of a tech nut, you'll be able to source virtual classes or activities too.

FOOD AND DRINK

You don't daydream or wake up thinking of food like some Earth or Water signs, and you have a contrary approach to nutrition — as you do to everything else! Why does everyone eat the same old things for breakfast, or eat pudding after dinner? You look at the accepted norms in eating habits and take them apart, which can result in some raised eyebrows from your loved ones. You may have studied nutrition very closely and have a better understanding than most about which vitamins and minerals you really need — and which to avoid.

You may have a very progressive attitude to food, eating a pure diet that focuses only on what your body requires, perhaps as a vegan or through practising strict calorie control. Green smoothies after fasting, unpronounceable vegetables from exotic countries for lunch, and a nut-based protein bar designed for astronauts if you feel peckish later. You're an unpredictable eater, and anything too samey drives you crazy after a while. This might result in some unusual fads, such as existing on caffeine until 3pm, then consuming only red food for two hours and then raw liver before bed.

DISOBEDIENT PATIENT

Naturally rebellious, it's not just food norms you'll question. You'll quibble over the knowledge and advice offered by most traditional healthcare givers. Besides, haven't they heard of emotional-freedom techniques, past-life regression or reflexology being the best for curing headache trouble?

You'll do your research obsessively, and if there's an outlandish theory that fits your current zany idea, you'll try it. Weirdly, the stranger a treatment sounds, the more likely it will be to work for you. And as the sign that's tuned in to the future, you have uncanny premonitions about which therapies might help you or your loved ones.

Aquarius's preferred places
- Singapore • Kennedy Space Center
- Kyrgyzstan mountains • Silicon Valley
- Tree-planting venture
- Sydney • Eden Project
- Icelandic geothermal power-station tour
- Angkor Wat • Area 51, Nevada

PISCES
(19 FEBRUARY — 20 MARCH)

You are Pisces, the Fish, the most compassionate and spiritual of all the zodiac signs, and your empathy is almost telepathic. Your zodiac symbol is depicted as two fish swimming in opposite directions, representing your constant flipping between fantasy and reality, and your immensely sensitive nature and boundless imagination mean it's sometimes challenging for you to feel rooted in the here and now. You're a deeply intuitive and emotional Water sign, reflecting the fathomless, mysterious power of the ocean, and sometimes you feel swept away on waves of feeling. You are ruled by elusive, ethereal Neptune, the planet of magic and illusion, and you have a reputation for being the most wonderfully creative person, even if you sometimes view the world through rose-tinted spectacles.

Each sign of the zodiac is thought to embody a little of the wisdom and lessons of the signs preceding it. As Pisces is the last of the 12 signs, you have absorbed all the wisdom, joy, pain and fears of the other zodiac characters. This explains why you have a rather blurred, obscure sense of self, and why you are more tuned to the collective psyche than anyone else. You're not entirely sure you want to be here, and as you contain the seeds of wisdom from all the other signs, on some level you feel like you may have already been here — seen and done it all already. Earthly reality can be beastly, and as a spiritually inclined Fish, you long to return to the ocean of universal consciousness.

ESCAPIST DREAMWORLDS

Much of your inspiration comes from your dreams or seems funnelled from a different plane of existence altogether. Your dream recall is usually incredibly detailed, often in full Technicolor with dramatic scripts and rolling credits before you wake up. Some Pisces remember the faces of people from their dreams so clearly that they would recognize them in the street. You're connected with levels of consciousness that the rest of us are not yet conscious of, and some Pisces can attain different states of awareness by meditating, through different sleep states or by just daydreaming. Sometimes you'll go anywhere just to get away from real life!

On some level you can't quite believe you have incarnated into this clunky, ugly world where everyone feels lonely. When you're tuned into other planes of existence, earthly life can feel heavy. Your desire for escapism is probably the most difficult for you to master, because why go through the effort and disappointment of finding a job, looking for someone to love, and taking care of yourself when you can get lost in books, sex or daydreaming? And, of course, there are alternate realities to be experimented with where you can blot out the real world completely.

Through identifying and empathizing with the challenging or dramatic experiences of the people around you, you will eventually realize that the reason you're here — and the lesson you need to complete your karma — is to help the lost and lonely souls in the world. And you can't do that if your own soul is flapping about listlessly looking for meaning!

LIFE'S CURRENCY

To make a dent in the physical world, you're going to have to get your head around money, which you'll see either as the root of all evil or as an elusive resource that

Most compatible love signs

SCORPIO You're one of the few people who can see past Scorpio's deadpan expression to the deep well of emotion inside — and you like it!

VIRGO Your opposite sign of Virgo gently and kindly shows you how to live in the real world without making it seem too unpleasant.

CANCER You're on the same level emotionally — both sensitive and careful with each other's hearts.

pours through you like water through a sieve. You can't say no to people in trouble, just as you can't ignore those heartbreaking television campaigns for animal charities or for people who desperately need help. You'll see one sad-looking doggy and give your last 10 pounds to an animal shelter before realizing you need it for rent!

It can take you quite a long time to figure out that money doesn't arrive or vanish on a whim. You have faith that money will materialize when you need it, mostly because that's exactly what it seems to have done in the past. But it's a pretty unreliable way to get along in life, and at some point you'll want some stability — a job, an address of your own and perhaps a family, pets or houseplants to look after.

Least compatible love signs

ARIES There's no sugar coating with Aries; they're as blunt and on-the-nose as they come. You need a bit more fairy tale and stardust than that!

GEMINI Gemini usually floats on the surface of things, when you like to dive in as deeply as possible.

LEO You need time away from people to feel like an individual, and Leo feeds off attention to feel like they're valid.

When you see what a difference your own money can make to help or care for other people, you'll feel more motivated to bring it in consistently. You are best suited to work where you are able to relieve others' pain or disillusionment, maybe in a job campaigning for a homeless charity, as a doctor or nurse, a psychotherapist or an alternative New Age practitioner. Your commitment to any deserving cause will shine through you and impress any employer with your dedication.

You'll also attract money by exchanging it for the wonderful manifestations of your rich imagination. But as you're inclined to underestimate your talents, you might need a little encouragement to get started. If you haven't already, you could begin by building an online audience for your astonishing art, fine dressmaking skills or marvellously inventive fiction.

YOU'RE WORTH IT

Not everyone is as open and understanding as you. You're a wonderful listener, and your empathic nature encourages others to share their secrets, worries and woes. And as you have an impressionable, boundary-less Neptune as your ruling planet, it's hard for you to separate your own thoughts and feelings from those of others. This is why it's important that you get enough time on your own to recover your sense of self. You have unparalleled skills for bringing beauty and happiness to others through your selfless deeds — and just by being yourself. But before you give yourself away, you must work on what it is that you love doing and what makes you happy. If you're going to inspire, uplift and encourage people who are confused about where they're going, you can't also be lost!

PISCES IN LOVE

Pisces is depicted as two fish swimming in opposite directions, simultaneously experiencing conscious and unconscious, heaven and hell. And nowhere do these extremes feel more apparent than in your love life. As far as you're concerned, the perfect union of romantic love is the closest to heaven you can be. You know that the merging of twin souls could make you feel whole again, perhaps because you've already had a taste of it in this life — or been there in a past one. Unconsciously or not, you wish for romantic love to save you, to swallow you whole and tell you that nothing else matters.

FISHY FAIRY TALE

You're so in love with love that you can't help but hope the next person you feel attracted to will prove all the fairy tales right. But that's a tall order for anyone to live up to. Your intended may even feel that you're looking right through them to some mystical reflection that bears little resemblance to her or him. If you're being realistic you might even feel, in some of your less limerent moments, that perhaps your reverence has very little to do with the flesh-and-blood person who just cooked you scrambled eggs.

HONESTLY, PISCES

When you care for others as deeply as you do it's essential that you try to see things clearly, and that's not that easy with ambiguous, hazy Neptune as your ruling planet. When you want something to be true, you'll often take the line of least resistance by pulling the wool over your own eyes rather than dealing with what's really there. You find confrontation hugely uncomfortable and will avoid asking loved ones direct questions for fear of finding out the truth. But that's exactly what you need to keep yourself rooted in the real world.

Honesty is what you need most from your relationships, because when you become more skilled at dealing with your own reality, you'll be a much better judge of other people's character and intentions — which should cut a heap of heartbreak from your life.

TRICKY EMOTIONS

You have an amazing ability to find beauty and magic in sadness and tragedy — and you can be strangely attracted to people who face real difficulties. But you'll need to have your reality head screwed on if you feel the line between compassion and romantic love beginning to get fuzzy. Go in with your eyes fully open and enlist some practical Earth-sign friends to keep your heart from slipping into fantasy mode.

PISCES AT WORK

You absorb the atmosphere of the pond you swim in, so your working environment is particularly important to you. In your younger years, you may spend time swimming from place to place, discovering what appeals and your preferred way of working. You'll probably have discovered that you prefer working quietly in the background. But anyone who thinks that because you keep yourself to yourself you're not doing anything of note is usually deceived. When it's your time to talk about what you've been working on, or your employer asks for results, you'll modestly render everyone speechless with your imaginative, well-thought-out piece of creative genius.

TRUTHFUL TACTICS

If you've been in the same job for too long, you may feel the waters stagnate, but as you dislike confrontation, you can become complacent and settle for the line of least resistance. Although it scares you silly sometimes, the truth is actually your greatest friend. Pluck up the courage to have a candid conversation with your employer if you feel things are going nowhere. You may be surprised to find that your talents will be missed, and that your job can be adapted or changed, reviving you with a refreshing new tank of water to swim in. Magical things happen when you turn to the truth, even when it feels so outside your comfort zone that it might break you in two.

FISHY CAREERS

You're the artist of the zodiac, able to communicate what cannot be otherwise expressed through paint, music, pottery, writing or fashion design. Your ability to take on your surroundings also means that you're a brilliant actor and mimic, so when you make a character study, you become the person you are focusing on. You'll feel at home in any job where you can use your extraordinarily rich imagination, and when your mind's in creative flow, it feels like you left a hundred tabs open on your internet browser. Visual ideas appear to download themselves into your mind from an invisible intergalactic portal.

The feet are associated with Pisces, and your graceful versatility might draw you to a career as a dancer, gymnast or ice-skater, and working in the charity sector affords you the opportunity to use your empathy and compassion for a good cause. If you feel you're making a difference to other people's lives, you'll probably stick around in that pond for years to come.

Perfect Pisces careers

• Artist • Chemist • Actor
• Dancer • Psychologist • Priest
• Swimmer • Chiropodist
• Nurse • Charity fundraiser

FISH AT THE TOP

You're an even-tempered, slightly reclusive boss, and responsibility can sit uneasily on your shoulders. Unless you have a smattering of workaholic Capricorn or Virgo in your chart, people come first. If someone on your team is sick or has to lend a hand in a family drama, you'll usher them out the door yourself, with instructions for bed rest or sincere wishes for their cat's welfare. And you live by the same rules. If someone needs you, they're your priority.

You are connected very closely to your team, and your mood will often change, reflecting the demeanour of the group as a whole. Just by walking past your team you can sense if there's something they're not telling you — and sometimes you would rather not know what that is!

Periods of self-employment can be a wonderful way to improve your self-discipline, as you'll have no choice but to stick to schedules and deadlines. You have a love-hate relationship with money, but when you're your own boss, procrastination no longer becomes an option; you have to keep on top of your own invoices.

PISCES FRIENDS AND FAMILY

You are a devoted, kind and compassionate friend who probably has a few friendships going back to at least school days. As a deeply compassionate person, you bend over backwards to make your friends, family, neighbours — and complete strangers — feel happy and cared for. You're strongly compelled to relieve suffering and, with such a giving nature, you're often found volunteering at your neighbourhood homeless shelter, organizing litter-picking sessions or adopting stray dogs and cats. You're quite a shy individual, but your intensely giving nature often sees you finding new friends at your many philanthropic ventures or at the local church, meditation circle or psychic group.

Your willingness to help can sometimes see others take advantage of your good nature, but you're so shocked at others' selfish motives that if you feel someone has taken you for granted, you'll swim as far away from them as possible, never to be seen again.

ASTONISHING INTUITION

Non-judgemental and a brilliant listener, you have an almost psychic ability to feel others' emotions, so you're right there with them through the happy or sad times.

You appear to be linked to invisible sources, and can sense when something is amiss. And as you often can't articulate exactly what, or use logic alone, to get your message through to the people you care about, you may instead quietly prepare to do what you can for them in anticipation of their world going pear-shaped.

You give without asking anything in return, and the people in your life come way before any practical concern, including being on time for work or eating regular meals. You're also unusually generous with money, which can leave you out of pocket when you really need it. You selflessly put yourself second — and sometimes third of fourth — but you soon learn that to have the energy to look out for everyone else, you need to make your own wellbeing a top priority.

PISCES AT HOME

Whether it's a metaphorical goldfish bowl or a luminous aquarium, your home will be tranquil and mysterious, with shimmering fabrics and reflective glass or crystal touches. You favour blues, greens and iridescent splashes in your decor, with sea-themed photography prints, ornaments and shells. A little chaotic by nature, your clutter seems to blend in with the rest of your possessions, and after a while you don't notice the difference! It's not that you're disorganized; you just like to have everything on show. Stuffed with art gear, musical instruments, sewing stuff and half-finished craft projects, your home's separate rooms blend into each other as one large creative, glittery glory hole. Throw in a few stray cats and dogs, and a couple of pals looking for a sofa for the night, and you'll have a Pisces paradise.

PISCES PARENT

Pisces parents will do most anything for their children. You know how to appeal to little kids' sense of wonder without ever needing a television or a computer game, as your storytelling is so vivid and believable. You can create whole worlds to inhabit, and you're almost as fond of them as your little ones are. At times a little absent-minded and detached, you can be forgetful about life's practicalities, such as laundry, regular dinner times or boring school homework, but who needs those when you have an imaginative Pisces around?

PISCES CHILD

Sensitive and thoughtful Pisces children often have a faraway look in their eyes, as if they're connected to the Moon or perhaps remembering a past life. Their boundless imagination can keep them entertained for hours, and they'll live in their favourite books and create magical worlds with just chewing gum and string.

HEALTHY PISCES

Graceful, delicate and a little shy, as an emotional Water sign you usually exist inside your emotions and your imagination. Ruled by magical but confusing Neptune, you may start off with good intentions about losing weight or exercising, but you become disillusioned when you don't see fast results, or start to feel uncomfortable.

Your imagination can be the most active thing about you, and because you're such a visual person, creating a mood board with images of people or clothes you like will help you keep on track. You might feel too self-conscious exercising in a group environment, or mortified by a personal trainer's close scrutiny, so going it alone at home or joining an internet class — without your camera on — should keep things more private.

Dancing is a much-loved Pisces activity, as it's linked with the feet — the Pisces area of the body. Like a fish shimmying through water, you're an elegant, gliding mover, and appreciate the finer aspects of dance, which can be lost on the Earth and Fire zodiac signs. And, of course, you're literally right in your element swimming and being in the water, and going for a quick dip in the ocean can feel like a religious experience.

LOSING YOURSELF IN FOOD AND DRINK

If you're feeling stressed or anxious, you can absent-mindedly use food as a way to stop you from focusing on what is really bothering you. You might even binge eat — and drink — to level out your changeable moods.

Your first instincts when not feeling great are usually Neptunian — and therefore escapist in nature. Turning to alcohol, chocolate or any mood-altering substance might work for a while, but unfortunately most of the addictive things in life aren't very good for you. Luckily, there are other, more satisfying ways to lose your mind... meditation, sex, even losing yourself in a book

Pisces's preferred places
- Spiritual retreat • Cinema
- Reading on the beach
- Stonehenge • Glastonbury tor • Bed
- Water park • Remote island
- The astral plane • Swimming with dolphins

FURTHER READING

www.astro.com This amazing astrological resource is extremely popular with both experienced and beginner astrologers. It's free to sign up and obtain your birth chart and personalized daily horoscopes.

GREAT ASTROLOGY BOOKS

PARKER'S ASTROLOGY
by Derek and Julia Parker (*Dorling Kindersley*)
THE LITTLE BOOK OF ASTROLOGY
by Marion Williamson (Summersdale)
THE 12 HOUSES
by Howard Sasportas (*London School of Astrology*)
THE ARKANA DICTIONARY OF ASTROLOGY
by Fred Gettings (*Penguin*)
THE ROUND ART
by AJ Mann (*Paper Tiger*)
THE LUMINARIES
by Liz Greene (*Weiser*)
SUN SIGNS
by Linda Goodman (*Pan Macmillan*)

ABOUT THE AUTHOR

Marion Williamson is a best-selling astrology author and editor. A former editor of *Prediction* magazine, Marion writes about astrology for heaps of magazines and websites. Twitter: @_I_am_astrology